*ne settlements*

*of Lake*

*Creek, and*

*and Crown*

*rnish many*

*necessaries*

*tate the*

*emy."*

LDIMAND

*Canada*

D0906518

# Carleton's
# Raid

# Carleton's Raid

IDA H. WASHINGTON
*and*
PAUL A. WASHINGTON

PHOENIX PUBLISHING
*Canaan, New Hampshire*

All quotations from the Haldimand Papers (the papers of
Frederick Haldimand, Governor-General of Canada) were
obtained through the courtesy of the Public Archives of
Canada. The originals of these papers are the property of
and are housed in the British Museum which has generously
granted permission to quote from the Haldimand Papers
(including Major Christopher Carleton's *Journal*) those
passages listed in the Notes starting on page 81.

Washington, Ida H.        1924-
    Carleton's raid.
    Bibliography: p. 92
    1. Carleton's Raid, 1778.  2. Carleton, Chris-
topher, b. 1749.  I. Washington, Paul A., 1953-    joint
author.  II. Title.
E241.C2W37        973.3'34        77-5739
ISBN 0-914016-37-7

Printed in the United States of America
by Courier Printing Company.
Binding by New Hampshire Bindery
Design by A.L. Morris

# CONTENTS

# INTRODUCTION

O N SATURDAY, October 24, 1778, at half-past six in the morning, an armed fleet commanded by Major Christopher Carleton left the Isle aux Noix in the Richelieu River and sailed up Lake Champlain toward the south. This armada was made up of two large vessels, the *Carleton* and the *Maria,* two smaller gunboats, a number of the long boats called "batteaux," and many Indian canoes; together they carried a force of 354 white officers and men and about 100 Indians. Their secret orders were "to destroy all the supplies, provisions, and animals which the rebels may have assembled on the shores of Lake Champlain, to take prisoner all the inhabitants who have settled there and have sworn allegiance to the Congress, sending their wives and children into the Colonies with orders not to return to that region."[1] Carleton was directed further "to destroy all the boats which he could discover, as well as all the sawmills and grist mills which could have been built there in the area."[2] Three weeks later the expedition returned to Canada with thirty-nine prisoners and the report that it had destroyed "4 months provisions for 12,000 men."[3]

The action was hailed as a major success by Canadian leaders, but American forces, then engaged in crucial battles far to the south, paid little attention to Carleton's invasion of the northern frontier. For the settlers whose homes were destroyed and whose men and boys were taken prisoner, the attack was a violation of the trust they had placed in "his Majesty's general officers' orders to stay peacibly on our several plantations and their promises that we should not be molested."[4] The Canadian reason for the attack, as given in a letter from Frederick Haldimand, the Governor-General of Canada, to the British Colonial Secretary George Germain, was that the action was necessary because "there are some settlements upon the borders of Lake Champlain, Otter Creek, and about Ticonderoga and Crown Point that may furnish many conveniences and necessaries which would facilitate the approach of an Enemy."[5]

Carleton's raid has received scant notice in volumes on United States history, and when the invasion is mentioned at all, the leadership is often mistakenly credited to one of Major Christopher Carleton's uncles, Thomas Carleton or Guy Carleton. Full Canadian accounts of that historical era are not plentiful, and there is only a small amount of Canadian published material about Carleton's expedition. Since the attacks occurred in an area which was sparsely settled and still relatively unorganized politically, the Vermont reports of the action were generally preserved as oral tradition and only written down several generations after the events.

Despite the lack of printed accounts of Carleton's raid, however, a rich store of unpublished documents has been preserved in the British Museum, with copies in the Public Archives of Canada in Ottawa. These include confidential instructions sent from the Canadian Governor-General Haldimand to Carleton and to those who were to aid him, detailed preparation plans, Carleton's own journal kept during the invasion, and subsequent letters and reports about the action, including prisoners' petitions for release, reports of prisoners' escapes, and finally directions for an exchange of prisoners.

When a mosaic is assembled from the bits and scraps of available information, the picture that emerges is a panorama of human experience against a background of primitive terrain and amid forces of historical and social change.

# Carleton's Raid

"This extensive Province, by which alone, in the present circumstances, at least as far as we know, Great Britain can seize fast hold of America, is, in its present condition, quite open to the insults and ravages of the Colonies in actual rebellion."

—FREDERICK HALDIMAND

# 1

## The Canadian Situation

IN 1759 the French and Indian War ended for eastern Canada, and by 1761 British rule had replaced French in all Canadian territories. This change in government involved much more than a change of leadership for the Canadians. Canada was already filled with nearly ninety thousand well-established settlers, whose cultural traditions, laws, and language were French and hence foreign to the new rulers. Outside of the two major cities, Montreal and Quebec, the French lived under a feudal system, consisting of a wealthy landed and military aristocracy, the "noblesse," and an illiterate, apathetic peasantry, the "habitants."

The French criminal code, which was uncompromisingly severe, and the paternalistic civil code, in which the "habitants" had no voice, worked together with a strong church organization to preserve order. The traditional British rights of trial by a jury of one's peers and of general participation and responsibility in civil government were unfamiliar to the new British subjects. Moreover, while the peace treaty finally signed between France and Britain specified religious toleration, British practice excluded Catholics from civil positions of responsibility, a limitation which created special problems in a land where the Catholic "noblesse" were the only experienced administrators.

There were perhaps as many as four hundred British civilians in Canada at the cessation of hostilities, but they were a group to whom

3

civil authority could hardly be entrusted safely. Traders, political and criminal fugitives from provinces to the south, disaffected soldiers, they were opportunists who would see in new civil positions a chance for personal wealth and would be little bothered by ethical scruples in acquiring it.

The new governors of Canada were charged with keeping order at home and resisting invasion from without while ruling a conquered people unfamiliar with British civil government, and with an organization of British civil servants corrupt from the beginning. Military affairs during the American Revolution were directed from England by Lord George Germain, the British Colonial Secretary, a man who had never visited the American Colonies and had only a vague idea of the geography and climate of the area under his command. His letters of instruction to his colonial administrators indicate that he envisioned the northern American colonies as an enlarged England, similar to the homeland in climate, terrain, and convenience of travel. Among his suggestions were recommendations that troop movements be made in the winter months when northern roads are generally blocked by snow and ice, that men be quartered in tents at seasons when temperatures regularly fall below zero, and that rapid troop movements be made over trackless terrain.

It was incomprehensible to Lord Germain that any person would not prefer to live under British rule if he were given free choice. It followed that the great majority of the colonial settlers must be loyal British subjects, and that quelling the American rebellion should require only the arrest of a small group of outlaws and terrorists. The result of this viewpoint was a refusal to provide the British commanders in Canada with supplies sufficient to wage war effectively. Germain limited materials and manpower to those appropriate for a minor and temporary police action, and he regarded requests for additional troops and supplies with great suspicion. Thus caught between the stubborn ignorance of their superiors and civil chaos among their subordinates, Canadian leaders of this period needed great persistence and ingenuity to keep their country intact.

Guy Carleton was appointed Governor-General of Canada in 1768 and had outstanding success in drawing the different factional Canadian groups together. He won the respect and cooperation of both French and British Canadians, but in his letters home he made little effort to conceal his contempt for the Colonial Secretary. As a result Germain ordered his removal, and he was replaced in June, 1778, by Frederick Haldimand. It was only after Germain's retirement in 1782 that Carleton returned to America, where he served as Governor-General of Canada from 1786 to 1796.

Frederick Haldimand, Governor-General of Canada from 1778 to 1786, was originally a Swiss soldier of fortune. His service in the British forces won for him the respect and confidence of the British government, and he rewarded this confidence by his able administration of Canadian affairs during this very difficult period.

It was no help to the governors of Canada, trying to rule a reluctant subject people, to have an active rebellion raging in the British colonies to the south. The spirit of insubordination was infectious, and those from the Colonies who crossed the border to spread the infection and make converts to the rebel cause were a constant irritation to Canadian authorities. On July 25, 1778, Haldimand sent a request to Germain for additional military help, complaining that his defenses were insufficient against infiltration from the south: "This extensive Province, by which alone, in the present circumstances, at least as far as we know, Great Britain can seize fast hold of America, is, in its present condition, quite open to the insults and ravages of the Colonies in actual rebellion."[1]

The most important military route between Canada and the colonies to the south was along Lake Champlain. The Champlain Valley had been of strategic military importance even before its discovery by Samuel de Champlain in 1609. The Algonquin tribes of Canada fought over the valley with the Iroquois nation, and it was with one of the Algonquin war parties that Champlain first entered the lake. The same year that Champlain discovered the lake which was named for him, Henry Hudson, on an expedition for the Dutch, discovered and claimed for the Netherlands the river which is his namesake.

In 1616 the English took over the Dutch colony of New Netherlands, a step which gave them control of the Hudson River. A glance at the map shows that a natural pathway through the wilderness between New York and Canada is provided by the Hudson River, Lake George, Lake Champlain, and the Richelieu River.

By 1778 the action in the Colonial rebellion had moved to the south away from Canada, but three years earlier Colonial forces under Montgomery had come north along the Hudson-George-

Champlain route and struck far into Canadian territory, and the memory of this almost successful invasion was still green in the Province of Quebec and its major cities. In the course of the 1775-1776 invasion, St. John and Montreal had fallen to Montgomery's forces and, with reinforcements brought in from the east by Arnold, Quebec had been placed under siege. When the British leaders pondered the threat of a new attack from the south, they recalled that during the earlier invasion the Canadians had remained largely neutral, neither helping the attackers nor fighting against them. It had been up to the British regular troops to repel the colonial invaders.

In October, 1776, the British defeated Arnold's lake fleet at Valcour Island and continued down Lake Champlain to take the fort at Crown Point. The following year Burgoyne's attempt to sweep the lake clean of rebels ended in disaster at Bennington and Saratoga. Now there were again active rumors of plans by Congress for another Canadian invasion, and secret Congressional records show that such plans were indeed made on December 3, 1777.[2] In the summer of 1778 a French fleet arrived in Boston, increasing the forces available for an attack against Canada. While the congressional plans for an invasion were abandoned on March 13, 1778, news of this decision did not reach Canada, and as late as October 18, 1778, Haldimand wrote to Germain, "Some People in this Province who were taken by Privateers in their passage with the Fleet last Spring and just lately back by Land, report that it was the language of the Country, wherever they passed, that an Army would soon make its appearance in Canada."[3]

It was not certain whether this invasion should be expected on the old Champlain route, or up a new path being blazed across Vermont from the east. A military road had been started in 1777 at Newbury on the Connecticut River. It was abandoned that same year in Peacham, with only about twenty miles cut through the forested wilderness, but the Canadians could see that if the projected path were extended it would shoot like an arrow across the Canadian border and towards a point on the St. Lawrence River between Montreal and Quebec. The originator of the road was Jacob Bayley, the founder of the town of Newbury, who had suggested to General Washington in 1776 that such a road be built so that troops invading Canada might be moved more easily through the northern forests.

Bayley personally supervised the building of the road as far as

Peacham, when Burgoyne's attacks put a stop to invasion plans for the time being. Bayley himself was appointed Commissary General of the Northern Department by Washington and saw action against Burgoyne at Saratoga. When the road-building project was renewed in 1779, it was under the direction of General Moses Hazen, who continued Bayley's road north-northwest to Westfield, as close as he dared to the British patrols on the Canadian border. The place where he stopped, now called Hazen's Notch, is about fifteen miles southwest of Lake Memphremagog.

The Vermont area had been settled by a group of pioneers respected and feared by the Canadians far beyond the strength of their numbers. Haldimand once observed that the Vermonters, "if once united with Congress, would be very formidable Enemies, having been from their Early Contests with their neighboring Provinces continually in Arms. They are in every Respect better provided than the Continental Troops, and in their principles more determined. These considerations, with the impossibility of acting from this Province except in great Force (owing to their inhabiting Champlain and George, Hudson and Connecticut Rivers, ready to a man to turn out upon the first alarm with provisions upon their Backs, and possessed of a Strong Country where they can attack and harrass a Corps in the most advantageous Situation), have always made me anxious to prevent the Union they seem so bent upon accomplishing . . . Such is the Enthusiasm of the Vulgar for their Idol, Independence, that nothing but unavoidable necessity will ever induce them to relinquish it."[4]

These neighbors were expected to give every assistance to a force attacking Canada. Repeated warnings had been ineffective in preventing settlement, and harassment by Indians and Tories, permitted and even encouraged by the British authorities, had not completely freed the northern areas of rebel settlers.

In July, 1778, Haldimand decided to launch a British attack on the Onion River valley (today called the Winooski) in northern Vermont. The immediate goals of this raid were to discourage the building of the Bayley-Hazen road from Newbury to the Canadian border, to rid the border country of rebels who might encourage the defection of Canadians, and to capture Hazen himself, who was reported to be on a scouting trip to the area.

Moses Hazen had lived in Canada, at St. John, for a while after the French and Indian War, but he had returned to the Colonies when

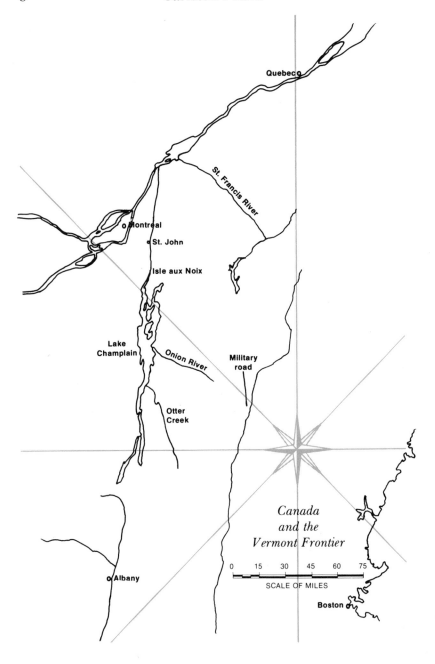

Quebec

St. Francis River

Montreal

St. John

Isle aux Noix

Lake
Champlain

Onion River

Military
road

Otter
Creek

*Canada
and the
Vermont Frontier*

Albany

0    15    30    45    60    75

SCALE OF MILES

Boston

the American Revolution began, and he supported the revolutionary cause heartily. His knowledge of the northern terrain made him an ideal choice to continue the Bayley Road northward, and hence a man to be particularly feared by the Canadians.

The man chosen to lead the Onion River raid was John Peters, a very different type of settler. Peters was doubly disliked by the Vermonters because he had sided first with New York and then with Canada. He had come from Hebron, Connecticut, to be one of the first settlers of the controversial area on the east side of Vermont which was granted by both New Hampshire and New York. There he had built a mill and had been appointed (by New York) justice of the peace, commissioner to administer oaths, and assistant judge and county clerk in the County of Gloucester. The authorities set up Kingsland (now Washington) as the county seat, though it was as yet totally unsettled, and Peters went with other officials on snowshoes to the area in February, 1771, to open court in the woods. When Vermont joined the rebellion against British rule, Peters went to Canada, where he raised a corps of Loyalists called the Queens Loyal Rangers and was given command of them with the rank of Lieutenant Colonel. He finally retired to England, where he died in 1788, and his Vermont properties were confiscated by the state.

Haldimand wrote to Lord Germain about his hopes that Peters might capture Hazen: "We have it from those who can be safely confided in, a Mr. Moses Hazen, well known in this Province, and who acquired some reputation in the late war, with a Canadian, settled at St. Francis, and four Indians, is come from Albany to work a road that way, which leaves very little doubt, they mean an Invasion of the Province, a party having already been sent that way to destroy the Harvest, orders are sent after them to hasten their march, could they lay hold of these gentry, the capture might prove of great advantage."[5]

The destructive force was to burn all those supplies and buildings in the Onion River Valley that might give aid to an approaching enemy. Haldimand prescribed the composition of the party to Peters thus: "You are for that purpose to take under your command and direction a Party to consist of one hundred men with proper officers from the different bodies of Royalists attached to the Corps of Mr. John Johnson; a small body of Indians will be added to your detachment for the purpose of scouring the woods and securing your march as you shall proceed."

He added specific instructions for the proper supervision of the Indians "in order to prevent entirely every act of cruelty or inhumanity from being committed by them."[6] On the day following this letter, another went out with the news that Hazen was on his way from Albany to St. Francis and urging Peters to "press your march" to intercept Hazen's route and capture him, with a reward of two hundred dollars for the capture of Hazen or his companion, the Canadian rebel Traversie.

Peters, however, was already having troubles with the Indians under his command. On August 11, 1778, he wrote, "By the misconduct of one of the Indian Battans Going to Onion River Last night the many Doubts arrising amongst the Indians in Executing your Orders — we have been Detained this Day. At 3 oClock this afternoon the Third Council was Held wherein the Savages Seemed Determined to Return. Captn. Horton used Every exertion to Shame them out of such Dastardly Conduct and on my Declaring by the Advice of my Officers that we Should Proceed If they Left us — they all Agreed to Go on Except fourteen Mohawks In case we would Return to Missisque Bay — and that I would Procure them a Supply of Rum to be at that Place on their Return.

"I beg your Excellency will therefore Order a supply of Provisions and Liquor if you think Proper. we Proceed To morrow morning." The letter concludes with the return address: "I am in the Woods."[7]

Peters did not capture Hazen, and the difficulties he refers to in his letter finally forced the expedition to turn back with only a small part of its mission completed. General Haldimand was determined nevertheless to proceed with his plan to destroy supplies and thereby make invasion of Canada difficult. The first mention of a raid on the shores of Lake Champlain and Otter Creek occurs in Haldimand's report to Lord Germain about the Onion River expedition:

"I informed Your Lordship in my letter of the 28th of July that I had sent a Party to destroy the Harvest in the Rebel Settlement nearest to our Frontiers. Owing to a disagreement between the Indians and the Loyalists Compy. composing the Party before they came near the spot where they were to act, they returned without fully answering the purposes intended, having only destroyed some Barns and a couple of mills upon the lower part of the Onion River, which, however, has obliged the People to abandon those parts and the Detachment suffered no loss. I mean still to prosecute this design, as there are some settlements upon the Borders of Lake Champlain, Otter Creek and about Tyconderoga and Crown Point that may furnish many conveniences and necessaries which would facilitate the approach of an enemy. I propose to send a respectable party, which will be covered by some of the ships and Gun Boats, and that it shall be as late as possible in going out as the Damage it may then do the enemy will be irreparable this season. The showing ourselves still on that side may probably have the effect of keeping up the difficulty which the Rebel Government is not without finding in enforcing obedience (an effect which is but too sensibly felt by us here, even from the insinuations of a few Agents of Rebellion) and the appearance of Invasion from where perhaps they do not expect it, may break or retard the measures of those people for carrying it to where they intend it."[8]

"*I propose to send a respectable party, which will be
covered by some of the ships and Gun Boats, and that it
shall be as late as possible in going out as the Damage
it may then do the enemy will be irreparable this
season.*"

FREDERICK HALDIMAND

# 2

## Preparations

THE ONION RIVER raid had failed because of trouble with the Indians. It was important to have a leader for the next expedition who would be able to command and direct Indians effectively. The man chosen was Major Christopher Carleton, the son of Guy Carleton's older brother William.

Christopher Carleton was born in 1749 at Newcastle-upon-Tyne. He was orphaned at four years of age when both his parents were drowned at sea, and joined the British army when he was only twelve. When he came to America, he lived for a time voluntarily among the Indians. A contemporary letter reports that "he went through all the severe ordeals they subject themselves to in order to show their fortitude, and had himself tatooed with the signs and totems with which they are accustomed to decorate themselves. He even went so far as to take a wife from among them, and he asserts that the hours he spent with them were the happiest of his life."[1] It is also told that he "dressed like a savage, painted his face, and wore a ring in his nose."[2]

For a young man with his family connections, Christopher's journey "back to nature" could be only temporary. He had two uncles in America, Guy and Thomas Carleton. Guy Carleton (1722-1808) was Commander of the British army in Canada from 1775-1777. He led the garrison forces at the siege of Quebec in May, 1776, and commanded the ships which destroyed Arnold's lake fleet at Valcour

13

Island the following summer. Subsequent disagreements with the
British home government brought about his recall to England early
in 1778. He returned later to be governor of Quebec from 1786-
1791 and 1793-1796. Thomas Carleton (1735-1817), Guy Carleton's
younger brother, was an officer in the Canadian forces and later
became governor of New Brunswick from 1784-1817.

It may well have been pressure from his distinguished family that
brought Christopher Carleton back from his Indian life into more
conventional paths, or it may have been physical disabilities, for his
health was not robust. He was greatly beloved by the men under his
command, both red and white, as this letter from one of the German
soldiers serving with him reports: "You cannot imagine a more
refined, gentle, friendly, well-mannered, and at the same time, a
more unaffected man than Captain Carleton; and although his
constitution has become wrecked and delicate, he still continues to
command the Indians who constitute our advanced guard, and by
whom he is greatly beloved. His present wife is a very handsome
woman, a 'my lady' and the sister of the wife of General Carleton."[3]

An amusing anecdote lies back of the unusual situation of a
nephew married to the older sister of his uncle's wife. In his biog-
raphy of Guy Carleton, A.G. Bradley tells the story thus: "Lord
Howard of Effingham, then a widower was a great personal friend
of (Guy) Carleton's, and of about the same age. On this account and
also foreseeing for him a distinguished career, he cordially accepted
his overtures for the hand of his eldest daughter, Lady Anne. She
and her younger sister, Lady Maria, had seen a great deal of Sir Guy
at their father's home, and doubtless regarded him as a benevolent
uncle rather than a potential lover. In time, however, they became
aware that other schemes were abroad, and on a certain occasion
when Carleton arrived at the house and was closeted with his Lordship it seems to have been pretty well understood what he had come
for. The two young ladies were sitting together in another apartment with a relative, a Miss Seymour, and when a message came to
Lady Anne that her presence was required by her father its purport
seems to have been well known. When this young lady returned to
her friends, her eyes were red from tears. The others, waiting
impatiently for her news, were the more impatient as well as
perplexed at her woe-begone appearance. 'Your eyes would be red,'
she replied to their queries, 'if you had just had to refuse the best
man on earth.'

"'The more fool you,' was the unsympathetic rejoinder of her younger sister, Lady Maria. 'I only wish he had given me the chance.'

"It appears that Lady Anne was already in love with Carleton's nephew, whom she afterwards married and who served under his uncle in Canada.

"There the matter rested for some months till Miss Seymour one day confided to Sir Guy what Lord Howard's younger daughter had remarked on hearing of his discomfiture. This so much interested the middle-aged lover, who, no doubt, had recovered from a perhaps not very violent passion, that in due course he presented himself as a suitor for the younger daughter, who proved herself as good as her word."[4]*

When Governor-General Haldimand chose Christopher Carleton, the nephew of his predecessor, to lead the expedition to Lake Champlain and Otter Creek, he thus picked a man who was close both to the highest levels of command and to the most troublesome and unpredictable of the forces under him. Christopher Carleton maintained throughout his leadership the complete cooperation of the Indians accompanying his forces, showing them always the respect and consideration one would exhibit to equal allies. At the same time, the morale and discipline of his own forces were high. These troops were the more difficult to command because they were made up of three very different types of personnel: regular British soldiers unfamiliar with wilderness fighting, German mercenary soldiers who had been sold into service by their rulers and were hence unwilling participants, and loyalists who had left the rebelling colonies and fled to Canada for a variety of personal and political reasons.

Traffic up and down Lake Champlain had long been active, and the shores of the lake were familiar to the Canadians. On July 27, 1778, a William Twiss wrote to Haldimand that "on both sides of Lake Champlain, there are a Number of Farm Houses many of which altho' abandoned, have several stacks of very good hay standing near them, and I daresay more will be made this Season:— perhaps it will be easy for the Vessels to bring such a quantity to St John as might supply the King's horses employed there."[5] This report of abandoned dwellings along the borders of the lake reflects

---

* Maria was subsequently known for the brilliance of her entertainment as first lady of Canada. She bore her husband eleven children and enjoyed in her old age the position of a distinguished and autocratic matriarch of a large clan.

the decision of many Vermont families to retire for safety to the protection of the forts to the south, returning for brief seasons, however, to harvest hay and store it for future use.

Some of the settlers had fled to Canada for safety, and these were a major source of information for the Canadians, but one which they did not entirely trust, for such "Loyalists" sometimes turned out to be men of colonial sympathies in disguise. On September 30, 1778, a group of Loyalists who had moved to Canada requested permission to return to get wheat and hay they had left behind.[6] This appeared to be a genuine request, but a letter from Brigadier General Powell to Haldimand just as Carleton's forces were starting out describes four other informers whose intentions were not so clear: "The four last Canadians give a very different account of the strength of the Rebels at Rutland from Mr. O'Neil. I hope you will permit me to keep them prisoners, till it is known whether their report is true. Should it be a false one, they must have some design in it, as they were some time upon the spot and ought to know exactly the state of the place."[7]

Canadian scouts and deserters from the Colonial army brought additional information. From the latter there were reports as late as October 28, 1778, after Carleton's fleet had already set out, of plans for an invasion of Canada, with descriptions of available supplies, fortifications, etc.[8] The scouts sent out just before the raid brought other disturbing reports. Every effort had been made to preserve secrecy, but on October 19, 1778, a letter from Frazer to Haldimand reported: "I am sorry to find that our destination (so far from being secret) is the public topic of conversation here in every Company & it is alleged by those who have lately been upon Scouts to the other side of Lake Champlaine that the rebels are informed that three hundred Indians were to be sent about this time to destroy the settlement along Otter Creek."[9]

Three officers were specifically directed in secret orders to supply Carleton's needs for the expedition. To Brigadier General Powell, who was in command at St. John, Haldimand wrote, "I am now to desire you will order seventy-five men from the 31st Regt. and thirty from the 53rd to join him with proper Officers, upon his requisition, provided with the quantity of ammunition and provision he may think necessary. He is likewise to be assisted with the number of Batteaux and Gun boats he requires, or any other thing he may deem requisite for the due execution of the enterprize committed to his charge. Secrecy in matters of this kind is ever to be observed, the parties therefore are not to understand they go further than the Isle aux Noix, and after their departure not boat or Canoe to be allowed to go up the Lake."[10]

To Captain Chambers, Haldimand wrote: "Major Carleton having received my orders and instructions to proceed up the Lake with a detachment of His Majesty's Troops; I am to desire you will give the necessary directions to the different Vessels under your command upon those waters, to be aiding and assisting to Major Carleton in the manner he shall point out to them, and to follow whatsoever orders he may think proper to give them for the advancement of His Majesty's Service."[11]

To Lieutenant Colonel Macbean, an aide of Haldimand's wrote: "His Excellency has received your letter of 16th instant, and will be glad to see you, whenever it suits your conveniency. Major Carleton having received instructions from His Excellency to apply to you for two Royals and two good Gunners, with proper quantity of ammunition and some Mantelettes, your supplying him with these things will be acting in conformity to the General's pleasure."[12]

A second letter from Haldimand to Powell enlarges on his instructions: "The principal object of Major Carleton's command being to destroy everything that can afford the Rebells resources upon the Lake, I am to desire the most profound secrecy may be observed on the subject; and to recommend to you to give him every assistance the exigencies of his situation may render necessary to demand from you. I have given directions to Lieut. Col. St. Leger to communicate to you every intelligence he receives of any movements of the Rebells, and to obey your orders in the mean time taking such precautions as his Judgement will suggest for the immediate security of his post."[13]

In September Powell wrote to Haldimand: "If your excellency would chuse to have any Indians stationd at that Post, Major Carleton informed me, he could get as many volunteers (who may be depended upon) as you please."[14] The Indians for the expedition began to arrive on October 21, 1778, and on October 24th Powell reported: "There are seventy two Indians gone with them, and Captain Lorrimer, who came to the Island after Major Carleton left it, says about twenty five of the Cachnawaga Indians, who were out a hunting upon the Lake, will join them, and that they were very ready to go upon his applying to them, and that they are very fond of the

Expedition."[15] Powell also sent with Carleton "one Smith, who was formerly in the Artillery . . . who was with me all the time at Tyconderoga, has a perfect knowledge of the country, and will be found a very useful man."[16]

Carleton himself added fifty-nine men beyond what was originally intended, an addition "which was occasioned by a requisition of that number of men to assist in working the Gun boats and guarding them and the batteaux after the Troops landed."[17]

The expedition was thus well equipped as it left Isle aux Noix before dawn on October 24, 1778. Powell, who watched the departure, wrote to Haldimand, "I will venture to say the Officers and men he has now under his command, are equal to anything which that number ought to attempt."[18]

"*This State is particularly exposed by its Contiguous
Situation to them to be first ravaged unless some such
effectual means shall be successful to prevent their
Invasions.*"

VERMONT COUNCIL

# 3

## Situation
## in the
## Champlain Valley

THE PERMANENT settlement of the Champlain Valley did not begin until after the end of the war between France and England for possession of North America. From 1756 to 1761 men from the New England Colonies fought side by side with British soldiers to drive the French from their fortifications on the shores of Lake Champlain and in Canada. The capture of Quebec and Montreal in 1759 and 1760 marked the end of active fighting, and by 1761 the colonial troops were released and could make their way back through the unsettled lands of northern New England to their farms in Massachusetts and Connecticut.

The main routes of return were through the valleys of the Connecticut River and of Lake Champlain. The land between these two bodies of water was claimed according to conflicting British territorial grants by both New Hampshire and New York. With the cessation of hostilities, each of these provinces was eager to secure its rights of possession by filling the disputed area with its own settlers. The grants made by each province were in accord with the pattern of settlement then in practice in each.

New Hampshire granted small, essentially autonomous townships, to be settled by independent farmers who managed their own political and economic affairs in the town meeting manner of the other New England colonies. New York, on the other hand, gave large manorial grants on which the land was to be worked by tenant

21

farmers as it was in the Hudson River Valley. The New Hampshire
grants were typically made to groups of speculators who resold the
land to people who would actually settle and farm it. The New York
grants were given largely to retiring army officers as a reward for
their service, and these in turn recruited new immigrants to America
to till the soil as their tenants.

The New Englanders who lived in western Connecticut and Massachusetts near the borders of New York had the opportunity to
watch these two systems of land management in operation and to
compare the lot of the farmer within them. As a consequence there
was no doubt among this group about which system they preferred.
The independent New England farmer changed and improved his
property as he wished, and through his voice in the local town
meeting he provided education for his children, roads for travel,
courts for the settling of local disputes, and militia for protection of
his property. The tenant farmer in New York feared to make improvements on his farm or dwelling because such changes could
bring higher rents or eviction in favor of another tenant. He and his
children were kept in ignorance by his landlord because illiteracy
helped to prevent disagreement with oppressive practices. The
courts and the military forces were brought in from outside and
served the interests of the landlords rather than those of the tenants.

In the Connecticut River Valley contact with New York practices
was infrequent, and hence there was less fear of New York land
ownership. The paradoxical situation thus arose that those most
eager to have New Hampshire grants of land, instead of deeds from
New York, were those farthest from New Hampshire itself. New
York never succeeded in establishing the machinery of government
in the Champlain Valley, while judges, clerks, and all the other court
apparatus functioned in the valley of the Connecticut River under
the auspices of New York. In fact, since much of the Connecticut
River Valley land had been granted by both New York and New
Hampshire, in some areas competing legal systems operated side by
side.

On the Lake Champlain side of Vermont, every attempt by New
York to certify claims to the land, either by sending in its own settlers
or by evicting those with New Hampshire deeds, met vigorous
resistance from the inhabitants, who organized a band of local
militia known as the "Green Mountain Boys."

Typical of the attitude of settlers along Lake Champlain toward the authority of New York is the story of David Wooster. Wooster had been granted by New York a tract of three thousand acres in the northern part of the town of Addison as recompense for military service. When he visited his property to look it over, he found a number of families already settled there, and when he returned with new leases under which they would be tenants to him as their new landlord, he was met by an armed group who "absolutely refused to accept, on any terms whatever," the leases he offered. When he then served them writs of ejectment, "they declared with one voice, that they would not attend any court in the Province of New York, nor would be concluded by any law of New York respecting their lands."[1]

The underlying causes of resistance to New York expansion into Vermont were sober enough, but the actual conflicts between the "Green Mountain Boys" and the "Yorkers" often had something of the flamboyant spirit of competitive sport played by overgrown boys. In 1771, when the sheriff of Albany County with an evicting party of four hundred appeared to claim James Breckenridge's land for New York, they were met by a large well-armed group of Green Mountain Boys, who watched with silent amusement as the sheriff's supporters melted away, and finally he also hastily retraced his steps to New York. On another occasion, when Dr. Samuel Adams of Arlington was found to be a New York sympathizer, he was suspended in a chair from the sign outside Fay's Tavern in Bennington and subjected to the taunts of the crowd.

A more serious confrontation took place at Vergennes, at the first falls on Otter Creek. A Colonel Reid of New York had been given a large grant near the falls in 1771, a place which had been deeded by New Hampshire ten years earlier. When Colonel Reid came in with his first settlers, he found the area already taken by about a dozen inhabitants who had occupied the shores of the creek and built a sawmill. He dispossessed these settlers, and in a subsequent complaint they stated that he "did take possession of one hundred and thirty saw logs, and fourteen thousand feet of pine boards, which boards were made in the same mill, and all lying thereby, all of which he converted to his own use. Not long after, the original proprietors of said mill did reenter and take possession thereof, but were a second time attacked by Col. Reid's steward, with a number of armed men, under his (supposed) instructions and by their superior force and threats, obliged to quit the premises again—all which tenements, said Reid occupied and enjoyed until dispossesed."[2]

The first tenants of Colonel Reid, who had added a gristmill to the settlement, were forcibly evicted by a party of Green Mountain Boys in 1771. Two years later, Colonel Reid again attempted a settlement, this time engaging several newly arrived immigrants from Scotland to accompany him to the territory, where they retook the buildings from the New Hampshire grantees, set up several new log huts, and repaired the gristmill. Reid brought in his settlers in June, and on August 11 a force of Green Mountain Boys, numbering over a hundred, descended armed on the settlement, informed the new settlers that they were trespassing and forced them to leave. The cabins were set on fire and burned to the ground, the gristmill was dismantled, and the mill stones were broken and thrown down the falls. The sawmill which had been built by New Hampshire grantees was, however, spared. Most of the Scottish settlers went over to the New York side of the lake to find refuge from the wild group of apparently lawless men who had dispossessed them. Two, Daniel McIntosh and John Cameron, however, elected to throw in their lot with the Vermont forces and received permission to remain.[3]

After evicting Colonel Reid's tenants for the second time, the Green Mountain Boys under the direction of Ethan Allen erected a blockhouse fort near the falls to prevent another attempt at settlement from New York.

The differences with Canada were disputed in a different spirit. To the Canadian authorities Vermont was the northernmost outpost of enemy country, and hence fair territory for any of the usual acts of war. In the borderland woods hostilities generally involved Indians, whose skill in scouting and knowledge of the terrain made them especially valuable to Europeans unfamiliar with wilderness conditions. The Indians were, however, always an unpredictable element to both attacker and attacked. The Indian customs of treating an enemy were, to Europeans, intolerably brutal and savage. Where the British officer proudly wore medals of valor on his chest, the Indian suspended scalps from his belt, scalps not too discriminately chosen between rebel and loyalist.

The problems of controlling the Indian forces used in military operations often proved insurmountable for British officers. The raid on the Onion River Valley failed because the Indians refused to cooperate with their foreign leaders. Often, as in this case, the British tried to bribe the Indians with gifts of liquor or guns, a practice which made the savages more dangerous to their British leaders as well as to the enemy.

It was the combination of Indians with raiding British forces that made these particularly dreaded by the new settlers in Vermont. With the Indians alone the settlers had practically no trouble. There was room enough, game enough, fish enough for all. Hunting and trapping parties of Indians often traveled up the river valleys, and as long as hunting and trapping and fishing were their sole business there seems to have been no conflict with the newcomers. The Vermont area had long been a hunting ground for local tribes and for some whose permanent settlements lay beyond its borders.

Indians in the employ of warring white forces were another matter, however, and the practice of instigating the savages to attack isolated settlements seems to have been widespread. The retaliatory actions of settlers in Vermont and particularly those of one man, Winthrop Hoyt of Monkton, who crossed into Canada repeatedly to stir up rebellion in the Indian villages close to the border, were one factor in bringing Carleton's forces into the Champlain Valley.

When British warnings and harassment were followed by an evacuation order from Vermont authorities, most settlers moved back to the forts in southern Vermont. They left behind crops still to be harvested, fields only partly cleared, and buildings unfinished. Some families stayed despite the dangers to complete these tasks; others left just a few of their hardier members to finish the summer's work before joining them in safety. The expected arrival of a new baby could also make moving difficult, and early Vermont records report a petition to the Council of Safety from David Bradley, in behalf of the inhabitants of New Haven and Ferrisburg, in which he "applies to this Council for liberty for their inhabitants to remain in their possessions at present, as by reason of the situation of some of the women it was impracticable for them to remove."[4] The areas along Lake Champlain and Otter Creek were thus only sparsely inhabited in November, 1778, and by a curious mixture of the hardiest and most daring and the weakest and most vulnerable among the settlers.

There was no question in 1778 that the danger of raids from the north was real. An attack on Shelburne in March of that year showed all the settlers of western Vermont what they could expect. There had been rumors in that area in January that an attack might occur, and the residents had sent a request down the valley for help.

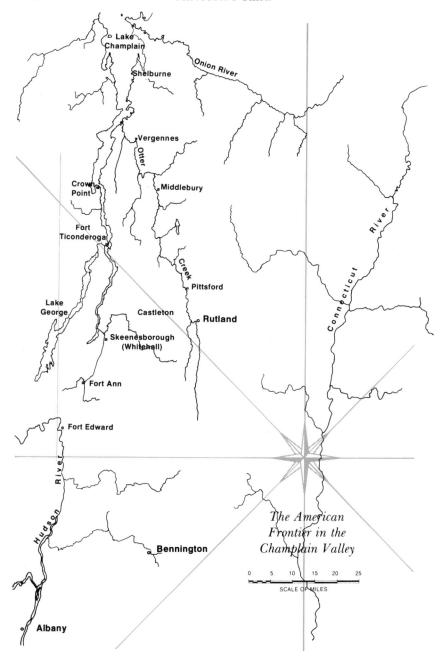

Lake
Champlain

Onion River

Shelburne

Vergennes

Otter

Crown
Point

Middlebury

Fort
Ticonderoga

Creek

Pittsford

Lake
George

Castleton

Rutland

Skeenesborough
(Whitehall)

Fort Ann

Fort Edward

Connecticut River

Hudson River

Bennington

*The American
Frontier in the
Champlain Valley*

0    5    10    15    20    25

SCALE OF MILES

Albany

Captain Sawyer of Clarendon brought a group of "minute men" seventy miles north through the deep snow and bitter cold. They stayed at the house of Moses Pierson and spent several weeks fortifying the house and preparing for the attack. Mr. Pierson had raised a large crop of wheat the previous summer, and early in March two men came to buy some of it, Joshua Woodward of Pittsford and Samuel Daniels of Leicester. About this time the people of Shelburne noticed that all the Tories were leaving the area, an indication that the time of the attack was near. It turned out that a Tory sympathizer named Philo had skated up the lake to Canada to lead back a force of British soldiers and Indians.

The attack came in the night of March 12, 1778, and both Woodward and Daniels were killed in the first volley of fire, as they slept in a room with an open window. The Indians set fire to the house twice. Lieutenant Barnabas Barnum of Monkton was killed in putting out the first fire. When the house was fired a second time, Captain Sawyer offered his watch to anyone who would extinguish the flames. There was no water in the house, but Mrs. Pierson had been brewing beer, and a large barrel of it stood available. One of the soldiers, Joseph Williams, took up the offer, cut a hole in the roof, and extinguished the fire with beer while bullets and arrows whistled about him, thus winning the watch. After the attacking forces withdrew, the bodies of a British officer and an Indian were found in a field near the house, and it was believed that other bodies had been dropped through a hole cut in the ice of the lake.

When the news of Barnum's death reached Monkton, his widow gathered her family of small children together and set off for Pittsford, thirty miles away, following the path by marked trees until she reached the fort.

Pittsford was the northernmost fort on Otter Creek, though there were blockhouses at Middlebury and Vergennes, and a house equipped with loopholes for the defense of the ford in Weybridge. The blockhouse in Vergennes, called in different accounts Fort William and Fort New Haven, was unoccupied at the time of the attack on Shelburne. Captain Sawyer was ordered to return to this fort after his successful defense of Shelburne.

His orders read: "To Captain Thomas Sawyer.—By Express have the honor of your Worthy exertions on thursday. While we regret the loss of Lt. Barnum and your men, Congratulate you on your Signal Victory over such a Superiority of numbers. Viewing your

dangerous and Remote Situation, the difficulty in Reinforcing &
supplying you, do therefore direct you to Retreat to the Block-house
in New Haven. Bring with you all the Friendly Inhabitants. You are
not to destroy any Buildings, wheat or the effects. You will remain at
sd Block-house until relieved by Captain Ebenezer Allen, or Capt.
Isaac Clark, who are directed immediately to repair to your Relief."[5]

The orders to Allen and Clark say that they are "to Take post at
Fort William, on Otter Creek, for the Time being. You will Send
Scouts to protect the Inhabitants, or to harrass the Enemy, as you in
your wisdom may Determine. All the inhabitants you cannot Safely
Protect, you are to Invite to move within your lines (to be by you
prescribed for the time being) within a Reasonable time, & all such as
move to Come in (if need be) you will assist, and those that Refuse
such kind Invitations, you are to Treat as Enemies to this & the
United States of America. If possible you will secure the Wheat at
Shelburn & such other effects as shall be in your power. You are not
to burn or destroy any Buildings, or other effects."[6]

The order "not to burn or destroy any Buildings, or other effects"
was in keeping with the plan of the Continental Congress to invade
Canada that spring. On December 3, 1777, the Congress had appointed Brigadier General John Stark to organize a secret expedition to go north on Lake Champlain to St. John to destroy shipping.
Another invasion of Canada from the east was to be simultaneously
undertaken under the direction of the Marquis de Lafayette. Colonel Hay was to be stationed at Ticonderoga and to raise troops in
Vermont in support of Stark. Hay's letter to Vermont received
immediate attention by the Council, which sent the following reply:
"Yours of yesterday date is now before this Council. They have duly
deliberated on your several requests contained therein, & in consequence have resolved to furnish three hundred effective men out
of this State exclusive of officers, who it is Expected will Engage as
Volunteers to Serve in the Northern Intended Expedition, who are
to continue in Service until the last day of April next unless sooner
discharged by the Commanding Officer of said Expedition . . ."[7]

In the effort to recruit soldiers from the east side of the Green
Mountains, a letter was sent on February 10, 1778, to several
captains, concluding: "As it is expected that a Respectable body of
Continental Troops will be employed in Conjunction with the Volunteers from this & the Neighbouring States, sufficient to penetrate
into Canada and thereby frustrate any designs the enemy may have

in a future Campaign of approaching this Country, and as this State is particularly exposed by its Contiguous Situation to them to be first ravaged unless some such effectual means shall be successful to prevent their Invasions, Therefore this Council flatter themselves, that no further arguments (need) be used to induce every well wisher to the Freedom & Liberty of himself & Injured Country vigorously to exert every Nerve on this most important Occasion."[8]

On February 15, 1778, a letter to Colonel Hazen, Commanding Officer at Albany, speaks of the necessity of having a guard at some post on Lake Champlain "for the purpose of securing the Hay & Forage Provided there for the use of the Army."[9]

On March 5 a request was read to the Council for protection of the inhabitants near Lake Champlain and Otter Creek, and on March 6 instructions were sent to Capt. Ebenezer Allen to raise troops and take post at the fort in Vergennes. From this post he was "to keep out proper Scouts to reconnoiter the Woods, to Watch the Movements of the Enemy, & Report them to this Council or officer Commanding the Troops in the Northern Department as often as you shall find from Time to Time necessary."[10] Before Allen could carry out these orders, however, the attack on Shelburne was made, and he was again ordered, on March 19, 1778, to go to Vergennes, where he could meet and relieve Captain Sawyer.

On March 13, 1778, the Continental Congress resolved to abandon the plan for the invasion of Canada, and Vermont remained open to attack from the north.

In answer to a request for protection from the people living along Otter Creek north of Pittsford, dated April 13, 1778, the Council replied on April 22 that "it does not at present appear to this Council, that we can Guard further North than Pittsford & Castleton. Therefore you will Conduct your selves accordingly."[11] A similar letter was sent on the same date to the people living in Panton, Addison and Bridport. Captain Ebenezer Allen was ordered to protect the inhabitants and to help them to move south to the safety of the forts, and Governor Chittenden's letter to him observes: "I have not the Least Doubt of your Military skill, & the Conduct & spirit of the officers & soldiers under your Command, & that with your exertions, in Conjunction with those sent to your assistants, you will be able (with the Blessing of God) to protect the Inhabitants against the fury and Rage of Savages & Diabolical Tories until Seasonably Relieved."[12] In sending out such troops, it was often necessary for them to live temporarily on supplies furnished by the local inhabitants, and the orders from the Governor and Council are specific that for each item taken a receipt must be given and a record kept, so that the settlers can be reimbursed for their support.

The fort at Pittsford remained the farthest north to be constantly manned by troops. Pittsford was the point where the Crown Point Road, built during the French and Indian War, crossed Otter Creek and divided, part going north towards Crown Point, the other part going more directly west to Fort Ticonderoga. After the Battle of Hubbardton in July, 1777, refugees and defeated soldiers streamed over the hills along the southern branch of the Crown Point Road into Pittsford, and the inhabitants of that town expected to find Burgoyne and his forces right behind the fugitives. Consequently some of the people of Pittsford fled south to the towns in Connecticut and Massachusetts from which they had come, and those who remained resolved to build a fort for protection in future emergencies. The fort they built was Fort Mott, which was arranged in a manner usual for such fortifications: the house of William Cox on the east bank of Otter Creek was in its center, and around this was set a high breastwork of hemlock logs. It was made "by the combined voluntary efforts of the neighboring inhabitants for their mutual security against the sudden attacks of roaming parties of Indians and British, piloted by the detestable renegade Tories, familiar with every road, by-path, log-house and ambush in the settlements."[13] The fort was named for John Mott, who commanded the garrison in it.

The peril of Indian attacks continued to be real, and on two different occasions boys were seized and carried into Canada from the Pittsford area. In September, 1777, Indians seized Joseph and John Rowley, fifteen and eleven years old, and a few days later Gideon and Thomas Sheldon, fifteen and thirteen, were taken as they brought a load of grain pulled by an ox team to the barn. After seizing the Sheldon boys, the Indians went on to the house where, a local chronicler reports: "As they entered the door Mrs. Sheldon, the mother of the two boys, in her fright sprang out of a back window. The Indians searched the house, took the only spare dress—a calico one—belonging to Mrs. Sheldon, and a web from the loom, partially woven, and retreated with their prisoners and booty. Mrs. Sheldon followed some little distance and entreated them to give up her sons but they refused."[14] Thomas Sheldon died in the

Canadian prison, but the other three boys were released and sent home after a few months' imprisonment.

About the same time, the house of Felix Powell nearby was attacked at night while Mr. Powell was away. It is reported that "Mrs. Powell apprehending an attack had fled into the thick cluster of bushes in the vicinity, and while there the house was plundered and burnt. In full view of the burning residence she was delivered of a child, before morning."[15]

News of incidents like these had spread down Otter Creek and along Lake Champlain, and recruiters had no difficulty in raising the promised three hundred volunteers to invade Canada. Vermonters could feel only disappointment and increased apprehension when invasion plans were dropped.

In view of the situation of the Vermonters in the fall of 1778, there is special poignancy in the first Thanksgiving Day proclamation, issued by Governor Thomas Chittenden on October 18, 1778. In setting aside November 26 as a "Day of Public Thanksgiving throughout this State," Governor Chittenden expresses not only gratitude for health and harvest, but also "for the Readiness of the People to stand forth in the Defense of their invaluable Rights and Liberties:—For divine Interposition in raising up a powerful Ally in Favor of the United States:—For every Instance of Protection and Success granted us and our Allies, both by Sea and Land, against our potent and inveterate Foes." He goes on to invoke Divine guidance for the temporal and spiritual leaders of the nation and state, and adds a plea "That Seminaries of Learning and Schools of Instruction may be, every where among us, promoted and succeeded." Specifically for Vermont, he asks "That God would yet make us glad, according to the Days wherein we have been afflicted, and the Time in which we have seen Evil:—That he would look down in Pity and tender Compassion on this State, in its Infancy; delight to own and bless it; and grant it may find Favor in the Sight of the grand Council of America:—That this once howling Wilderness may, in a spiritual Sense, bud and blossom like the Rose:—That he will be pleased to bless and prosper the Work of our Hands:—Establish his Covenant with us and our Children to the latest Posterity."[16]

Before the day appointed for thanksgiving arrived, Carleton's fleet sailed up Lake Champlain, and for the settlers on the shores of the lake and on the banks of Otter Creek a generous measure was added to "the Days wherein we have been afflicted."

*"It requires more patience to conduct Indians than most Gentlemen are possest of."*

CHRISTOPHER CARLETON

# 4

## The
## Expedition

ON THE MORNING of October 24, 1778, at five o'clock, Major Carleton wrote to General Haldimand: "Every thing is ready & the men are parading to embark."[1] Brigadier General Powell watched the fleet depart and reported that "no men could go off in greater spirits."[2]

The men must have needed all the enthusiasm they had to deal with the discouraging weather which chilled and dampened them for most of the next week. Carleton's journal lists "Wind fresh down the Lake with small rain,"[3] followed by wind which "blew so fresh from the S.W. that it was impossible to Stir."[4] Then, after a brief respite, a northeaster struck the lake, "so exceedingly fresh it was imposible to get our Boats of the Shore,"[5] and this storm continued for thirty-six hours.

The force which was commanded by Carleton contained officers and men from the 29th, 31st, and 53rd Regiments, the 29th Rangers, the Royal Regiment of New York, and the Royal Artillery. By ranks there were 1 major, 7 captains, 10 lieutenants, 3 ensigns, 1 surgeon, 15 corporals, 17 sergeants, 5 drummers, 4 matroses (gunners), and 291 privates.[6] This made 354 in all, drawn from British regular forces and American loyalists, augmented by German mercenaries; these were accompanied by about 100 Indians.

The years of living among the Indians had given Carleton understanding and respect for their ways, and he consistently treated them as equals. Too many of his fellow officers courted disaster by

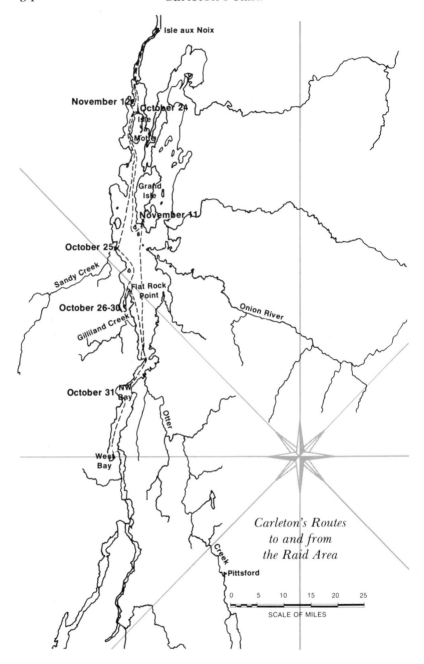

Isle aux Noix

November 12    October 24
                Isle
                La
                Motte

Grand
Isle

November 11

October 25

Sandy Creek

Flat Rock
Point

October 26-30

Gilliland Creek

Onion River

October 31   NW
              Bay

Otter

West
Bay

*Carleton's Routes
to and from
the Raid Area*

Creek

Pittsford

0      5      10      15      20      25

SCALE OF MILES

bribing the Indians with guns and liquor, or regarded them as children who must be held to a standard of subject obedience. On one occasion, when Carleton discovered a situation of mismanagement of Indian affairs, he reported it to Haldimand and suggested that the British representative with the tribe be changed, observing that "it requires more patience to conduct Indians than most Genln are possest of."[7]

With Carleton as leader, there was no problem in recruiting a suitable number of Indians to accompany the expedition. Powell reported: "There are seventy two Indians gone with them, and Captain Lorrimer, who came to the Island after Major Carleton left it, says about twenty five of the Cachnawaga Indians, who were out a hunting upon the Lake, will join them, and that they were very ready to go upon his applying to them, and that they are very fond of the Expedition."[8]

During the raid, the procedures and plans were changed several times because of advice or complaints from the Indians. The first stage up the lake to Isle la Motte in wind and rain brought objections from the Indians, whose journey in open canoes must have been a very uncomfortable one. Carleton had hoped to go further, but he waited for them, delaying his attack because, as he reported, "I feared if I went on without them they might turn back, as I was inform'd they were not pleas'd with coming so far the night before."[9]

Major Carleton traveled on the ship Carleton, a sailing vessel named for his distinguished uncle Guy Carleton. A comparable ship, the Maria, was already waiting at the mouth of Gilliland Creek (Bouquet River) on the New York side, and the gunboats were sent ahead to wait there, too. Carleton stopped a little farther north, at Sandy Creek (Ausable River), and set up a camp.

The first contact with a settler was made here, when a Mr. Campbell "came in haveing seen the Gun Boats as he was padeling in a small Canoe along Shore."[10] The news he brought was not encouraging: "He inform'd me that for certain I had been expected five weeks before at Rutland, that Whitcomb's post was Augmented to five hundred men, that Colonel Warner with two hundred was at Fort Edward, and that all the Militia was orderd to be ready at a moments Warning."[11]

Such information made it necessary to send out scouts before continuing the attack, but the wind from the southwest was so strong that it was impossible to launch a canoe. While thus delayed in his progress, Carleton improved the time by ordering a field day "to practice the men in the Wood fighting &c."[12] British soldiers were notoriously inept in their encounters with American woodsmen, and it is a sign of Carleton's realistic appraisal of his forces and situation that he gave them this kind of practice.

Carleton's own report of what he did next gives a good picture of his methods: "After the field day I assembled the Indians Chiefs and told them my wish to send a person I could confide in to bring me a true State of the Strength and situation of the Enemy. They saw the propriety of my proposal and consented to send the person I should pitch on for that service, in a small Canoe with five of their Young Men who were to go up with out loss of time to the Vesel at Crown point, there remain untill dusk and under favour of the Night land him wherever he should think proper and return to the Vesel before light come down the Lake and Joyn me in the Evening. The person I sent was Mr. Johns, and at his request a Serjant of Captains Sherwoods Company with him. They expected to be in four days from their landing back at the place they sett out from; I made them lye down in the Bottom of the Canoe cover'd them over with a Blankett that they might not be seen."[13]

After sending the scouting party off on Tuesday, October 27, Carleton had "intended to have moved off at dark,"[14] but the wind arose again, this time from the northeast and blew up such a gale with heavy rain that he was held inactive until Thursday the 29th. Early that morning the winds subsided, and Carleton again ordered a field day while he waited for dark. In the afternoon the canoe which had taken Johns returned with the report of seeing "a Rebel Canoe" which they had chased into the bay behind Crown Point but had not been able to catch. He also reported that the Maria had, contrary to orders, moved across the lake and north to the mouth of Otter Creek. The Maria had been stationed at Crown Point to discourage local traffic on the lake and thus to make it possible for Carleton to approach unnoticed with his other vessels so that his attack would be a surprise. He ordered the Maria back up the lake to Crown Point and "requested the Chiefs to send two Scouts."[15] One was to wait at Crown Point for Johns, in case he returned before the Maria got back there, and the other was to try to intercept the rebel canoe which had been seen by Johns' party.

On the 29th the expedition suffered a casualty, when a soldier of the 29th Regiment was killed by a falling tree. On the 31st the two

Indian scouts returned, but with no information. Carleton determined to set off up the lake that evening, but "the night was so remarkably clear that I could not venture to sett off untill past twelve."[16] He then proceeded southward up the lake, passing the *Maria* within half a mile, but so silently that he was not perceived, and anchored in West Bay behind Crown Point.

Carleton informed Mr. Alder, the commander of the *Maria*, of his arrival, and Alder replied that he had seen some people near a house on Chimney Point and had brought them off. "They proved to be four Inhabitants of Otter Creek Daniel McIntosh, David Stowe, Nathan Grizell, and James Henderson. I directed that they should be detain'd Prisoners on Board, as I knew they could come there for no other purpose than to pick up Intelegence. I went on board to examin them but could not get any thing out of them. McIntosh I have since found told me very Great untruths, and he knew them to be such at the time."[17]

Daniel McIntosh had been one of Colonel Reid's Scotch immigrant settlers at the first falls of Otter Creek (now Vergennes). When Ethan Allen and the Green Mountain Boys had descended on the little settlement and chased most of the inhabitants back across the lake, McIntosh was one of two who asked permission to stay and join Allen's forces. He had evidently done so wholeheartedly, for he was clearly keeping watch on the lake with neighbors from farther up the creek, Griswold (here Grizell) from what is now Waltham, and Stow from Weybridge. Henderson's name does not appear in early Vermont records, and so his exact home location is uncertain.

Carleton's encounter with McIntosh had been intensely irritating. His next attempt to question a Vermont settler was even more frustrating. In his journal he wrote: "Monday the 2d Novr. sent fresh Scouts to different parts of the Country. at twelve one of them returnd with a Benjamin Everest, I desired him to be conducted to the main Guard, and that no person Should be allowed to come near or Speak to him. I followed in less than five mints but before I reach the Guard he made his escape I made use of every means to catch him but without Success."[18]

The key to Benjamin Everest's sudden disappearance is provided by Vermont records, where we find a colorful, if not wholly accurate, account. Abby Hemenway's *Vermont Historical Gazeteer* reports that Everest, who was the commander of the fort at Rutland, went as a spy to Crown Point, where Carleton's ships had stopped for repairs. There he was recognized by a Tory neighbor named Benedict and was taken prisoner. After nine days on shore he was transferred to one of the ships, where he found thirty-nine other prisoners, most of them men he knew. The ship stopped at Fort Ticonderoga to take on supplies, and Everest was able to bribe a sailor to bring him a bottle of liquor.

That night there was a severe snowstorm, and a tent was set up on the ship's deck to shelter the prisoners. Everest invited the sentry into the tent to share his liquor and then stepped out himself to survey the storm. Slipping into the icy lake water, Everest then swam to the bridge which spanned the lake and climbed up on it. A fellow prisoner Spalding, who was to go with him, turned back when he felt how cold the water was, and so Everest escaped alone. At the east end of the bridge a group of British soldiers was camped, while the west end was guarded by Indians. Everest chose to go west, hoping to pass the Indians in his Tory disguise. Unfolding the razor which he carried in his pocket, he crept between a sleeping Indian sentry and a quantity of goods piled ready for shipping, "ready, if the man stirred, to cut his throat." Then he made his way past the Indian camp and northwest into the hills.

About sunrise he reached Put's Creek and shortly afterward found his friend Webster chopping wood. From the high land on the west side of the lake, Everest and Webster watched the movements of the fleet, and after dark Everest used Webster's canoe to return to the east shore of the lake, "giving the fleet a wide berth."[19]

The inaccuracies and anachronisms in this story are many. There was at the time of Carleton's expedition no garrison at Ticonderoga and no bridge across the lake. Carleton's ships did not put in for repairs at Crown Point, and most of the other prisoners (only thirty-nine in all) were captured after Everest. Like other pieces of oral tradition, however, the account of Everest's escape probably rests on a true incident, and it seems likely that he did indeed swim to safety, even if not in just the manner described in the Hemenway account.

Benjamin Everest was a lieutenant in the Green Mountain Boys, with a record of the kind of daring and successful encounters with Indians and British that give rise to legends, and it would be entirely in keeping with his character to slip away from his captors by swimming the icy waters of Lake Champlain. The Webster of the Hemenway account may well be the same Benjamin Webster whose name appears on the list of prisoners in Quebec as taken on Lake Champlain, November 7, 1778, that is a few days after the escape of Everest.

Everest was brought in by one group of Indians. Others sent out at the same time did not come back until the next day. Carleton wrote: "A Scout of three Indians which I had sent to the mountains opposite my Camp Saw two Rebels on the Top of one of them, but could not take either of them."[20] It is interesting to speculate that these could have been Everest and Webster, watching the movements of the fleet.

Carleton was sure, now, that his expedition had been discovered, and so he again called the Indian-chiefs together to consult on the best course of action. The plan which he laid before them was this: "In the uncertainty I was in relative to the Strength of Whitcombs Fort, I would not touch it, but thought it advisable for me to march with Greatest part of my detachment by a route which I knew would carry me in upon Otter Creek, thirty miles above the mouth, from whence I should proceed downwards, that I wd send Captain Fraser with thirty of their Young Warriors and 30 Rangers who should move up towards Pittsford destroying as they went on so that when they found it expedient to retire they would be Able to march much faster untill they overtook me than any party sent in their pursuite could in prudence attempt."[21]

Carleton's plan found approval with the chiefs, and preparations were made for departure the next morning. About midnight, the officer Johns, who had been sent out six days earlier, returned with the information that "there were three hundred Men at Rutland and two hundred at F. Edward, that the Arms of all the Inhabitants on the Creek were assembled at the BlockHouse, and that there were Seven hundred half Pounds of Powder with a proportion of Ball for that number of Militia in case of necessity, that Whitcomb had 44 single men as scouts on the different parts of the Lake but that there was not the smallest mention of our approach."[22]

This new information made another conference with the Indians necessary. Carleton reports: "I was up by day light, Assembled the Chiefs and communicated the information I had received, which put them in Great Spirits about the plan determin'd on the Night before only they thought it most advisable, not to sett off untill the dusk of the Evening."[23]

During the day scouts came in reporting that they had sighted rebel canoes carrying about thirty men each , but had not been able to intercept them, and also that they had seen smoke at the sawmill near Ticonderoga. Lieutenant Houghton and some Indians were sent to Ticonderoga with instructions to take a prisoner. The next day he returned, having been able to discover no trace of fires or people where the smoke had been seen, but with a new report of seeing with his spyglass on the opposite shore near the place where the canoe loads of rebels had eluded them the day before "the stern of a Batteau which was drawn up into some bushes in the deep Bay" and "two Men with Arms walking on the Beach."[24]

Then a message came from Lieutenant Alder, the commander of the Maria, reporting "that at one oClock, seeing a Canoe at one Smyths House on the East Shore two miles from Chimney Point he went in his Boat to enquire who she belonged to. Smyth came running down to the Water side and requested Mr. Alder not to land for that Scouts from Whitcombs Party at Ty. had left the House about twenty minnets before."[25]

Carleton "sent off fresh Scouts on each side the Lake with directions not to return untill they had either taken a Prisioner or were certain there were no detatchments there."[26]

He also sent a force consisting of an officer and thirty men to capture Smyth and bring him in for questioning and to set up a post near his house to surprise any force coming to it. This force he kept covered further by having the two gunboats move up to a position just off shore.

When Smyth was brought in, he told Carleton "that a Lieut. Crook with one Ensign and twenty five men had come there in two Boats the Night before, that they had a Birch Canoe with them which they Said they took that day from an Indian Scout, they Staid untill twelve oClock the next day at his House and haveing hid their Boats and Canoe, in a Creek close to the House were gon four Miles down the Lake that they Should be back that Night that they were detatch'd from a Party which Whitecombe had near Ticonderoja."[27]

Carleton "Suspected very much the truth of all this Story as it was evident those Boats with the twenty five men were the two Boats with Sixty which the Indians said they had been pursued by, and it was evident by their comeing in Boats they had come from Skeansborough and not Rutland."[28] To interfere with any action that the enemy could be taking, Carleton immediately dispatched, at two A.M., a force in pursuit. As he always did, Carleton acted with the knowledge and cooperation of the Indians. He reported: "I orderd a Captain with two Subalterns and forty Men with forty Indians to go off imeaditly to Surprize this party on their return; the Chiefs on being inform'd of my intentions agreed to it without hesitation and the Party under the Command of Cap. Dixon of the 29th Regt. and Captain Fraser with the Indians sett off at two. At two in the Afternoon the detatchment return'd, had been Seven Miles down the Lake but could not overtake the Rebel Scout as they had Struck off into the Woods towards Otter Creek and were twelve hours a head of them. They brought in fiveteen Prisioners Inhabitants on the Lake."[29]

The Vermont record of the capture of Smith differs in a number of interesting details from Carleton's report. It reads: "Not long after Mr. Smith and his family took up their residence here, such uncertainty, disquietude and unsafety arose among the settlers, in consequence of the quarrel between the government of the province of New York and the people of the 'Grants,' and especially upon the reception of the news of the approach of Burgoyne's army, in 1777, that most of the families in the town, especially those who had settled on or near the shore of the lake, left their homes and moved to more quiet localities. A few remained, however, and among the number was the family of Mr. Smith. Although frequently annoyed by the impertinent demands and hostile demonstrations of the 'York State men,' they succeeded in maintaining full possession of their domicile, living in peaceful and friendly relations with the Indians, who frequently visited the settlement, until a short time previous to Carleton's raid in 1778. On receipt of the news of the approach of that irregular and destructive band, Mr. Smith's family, with the exception of Nathan and Marshall, after selecting what articles could be best carried on their backs and in their arms, the bundles being apportioned according to the strength of each, left their home and started through the forest to the stockade forts at Pittsford, in Rutland county. Nathan and Marshall remained for the purpose of securing, if possible, and secreting the fall crops which were then on the ground. The family left in September, though the hostile party did not actually arrive until the 1st of November. On the 4th of that month Nathan and Marshall, with a man by the name of Ward, were captured and taken to Quebec, while improvements and buildings erected in the settlement were destroyed by fire, one dwelling only in town escaping the general disaster."[30]

While the force sent by Carleton down the Vermont side of the lake was busy destroying buildings and rounding up prisoners, the scouting parties sent to the New York Side "returnd without seeing any appearance either by tracks or Fires of any party haveing passd that way."[31]

A new consultation with the Indian chiefs was now in order, and as a result of this discussion the original plans were significantly changed: "I assembled the Chiefs to know if they approved of our setting off the next morning, and would attempt the execution of the first plan or thought it Necessary to adopt a new one. They would give me no answer untill they had consulted their young men that it was too late to let me have the answer that night but that I should have it next morning...I was up before day, Assembled a Councill and demanded their answer they said they thought it would be imprudent to Strike higher on the Creek than where I had propos'd going myself that they would go there if I would promise to take care of their Horses, which I consented to so far as lay in my power, they desired to know what I would allow them a Head for the Cattle that might be taken. I told them Eight Dollars for large Oxon, and in proportion for smaller Ones. I consented to this in hopes it would prevent them from amusing themselves about other plunder & recommended the women and Children to their care to leave provisns for them."[32]

While these plans were being set up, two German soldiers, one of the 31st and one of the 53rd Regiment, deserted in the night. Carleton "sent after them & promised a reward but they got clear off."[33]

In a letter on the American side from Colonel Alexander Webster of the fort at Skenesborough (now Whitehall) to Governor Clinton, we learn more of the fate of the German soldiers who left Carleton's force: "one Capt. Allen was at Crown Point when my Scout was their, and he found two Hessians that had Deserted from the Enemy; they had been Eight Days wanting Vitles & they give Much the Same account about the Enemies behaviour & say that the hellish band was about Six hundred in number & that their is three regiments in Canada & that the Enemy talked of penetrating further Into the Country; they say that S. Johns is Strongly fortifyed & the Isle of Noix."[34]

With the agreement of the Indians, Carleton was ready to send a considerable force inland from the east shore of Lake Champlain to

Otter Creek. They would proceed east across uninhabited terrain from a point two miles south of Chimney Point to Otter Creek, and then move north along the creek to its mouth, destroying buildings and supplies and taking prisoners in a series of surprise attacks.

The force sent out included "two Captains, five Subalterns and one hundred men with Captain Jones and twenty Royalists for this expedition. Captain Fraser Lieut Browne and Lieut Houghton with the Indians: the two Mr. Frasers went as Volinteers. Captain Ross of the 31st Regiment as the senior officer on this expedition Commanded it."[35] They landed at two in the afternoon of November 6 and "sett forward imeaditly."[36]

The invasion of Burgoyne in the summer of 1777 had so alarmed the inhabitants of the settlement on Otter Creek at Middlebury that all had fled their homes to seek refuge behind the fortifications to the south. The settlement was just becoming well established when it was abandoned. There was a blockhouse by the ford above the falls, and a schoolhouse had been built in the southern part of the town, where the first session had just begun with Miss Eunice Heep as teacher. A resident who took part in the exodus as a child remembered later how "her mother went out, before they left, among the garden vines, which were numerous and promising, regretting to leave them," and that a neighbor who remained longer reported that he "had visited her mother's garden after the family had gone and found the melons ripened by thousands."[37]

Carleton's force probably reached the creek within the present limits of Middlebury, for the houses of Joshua Hyde, Bill Thayer, and Robert Torrance in the south part of town were left untouched. They found the settlement empty and turned north, destroying all the buildings and supplies along the creek except one. Colonel John Chipman had recently erected the frame for a barn of green timber. This "they could neither burn or chop down,"[38] and so left standing, and when Samuel Swift wrote his history of Middlebury in 1859, he could still see the "marks of the hatchets on its timbers."[39]

The British forces went around the five falls in and just below Middlebury and came to the valley lands of Weybridge, where a number of settlers' cabins had been built on the banks of Otter Creek. The first settler, Thomas Sanford, had come with his wife and a son and daughter some time before 1775. He had built a cabin near a bend in the creek below the falls on the west bank, but later he left this first cabin and built another at the junction of Otter Creek

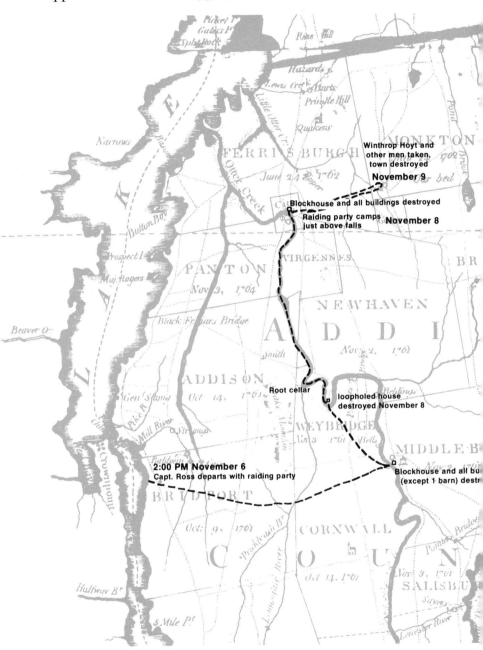

*The Otter Creek Foray/November 6 to November 9*

and Lemon Fair.[40] There he dug a large cellar into the creek bank
for the storage of vegetables during the winter. His son Ira was the
first child born in Weybridge. After Sanford built his second cabin,
Claudius Brittell and his family moved into the first, and about the
same time David Stow and Justus Sturdevant settled a little farther
up the creek on the east side. The Sturdevant cabin, at a shallow
place where the creek could be forded, was loopholed for defense.

All these settlers had remained in their cabins in spite of rumors of
imminent attack, so Carleton's forces found all the dwellings of the
little settlement occupied. David Stow and Thomas Sanford had
already been taken prisoner, but Stow's son Clark, Sanford's son
Robert, Justus Sturdevant, Claudius Brittell and his son Claudius
were all captured at their homes and led away. While Carleton's
report mentions Sanford and Stow among those captured "near
Crown Point,"[41] a local history gives a different account: "David
Stow, and Thos. Sandford, a near neighbor, had gone to Crown
Point, to mill, in a canoe. This took them down the creek to the falls,
a distance of 9 miles. Here they took their canoe and grist around the
falls, and then proceeded to the lake, 8 miles further. They then
passed up the lake, and crossed over to Crown Point. The route
could not have been less than 30 miles. They were returning with
their grist, and had got above the falls, when they were met by the
marauding party, captured, and with their grist taken on with the
rest of the prisoners and booty."[42]

Robert Sanford, the youngest captive, was then ten years old, and
after the party had gone only a short way he collapsed and was left by
the wayside. He made his way back to the other survivors, and they
all took refuge from the weather in the root cellar dug by Thomas
Sanford into the creek bank, for all the houses had been destroyed.
During the next ten days they subsisted on potatoes stored in the
cellar, until they were rescued by American soldiers. Local tradition
reports that Robert Sanford set out barefoot along the icy banks of
Otter Creek toward Pittsford, the nearest fort, which was twenty-
five miles upstream, and that he met the soldiers who were looking
for survivors of the raid and directed them to the cellar where his
mother and the others were hiding. The soldiers took these survivors back to Pittsford, and they remained there or went farther
south, not returning until the end of the war.

From Weybridge the raiders continued down the river through
New Haven and Waltham, where several brothers named Griswold

had settled. Nathan Griswold (Grizell in Carleton's report) had been taken prisoner on the edge of Lake Champlain, but Adonijah, David, and John Griswold were all captured in the valley. Their father, John Griswold, Sr., was also taken, but was released because of his advanced age. A local report tells also of a younger son: "Doctor Griswold, the youngest son of John Griswold, Sen., then about 7 years of age, was left by the foe with the women. An Indian came into the house of his father, in search of plunder. He espied a pair of new shoes, belonging to little Doctor, on a shelf, and bagged them. This act of robbery obliged the little boy to go to Manchester barefoot, over roads abounding in stumps and roots, his feet exposed to the frosty air of November."[42]a

Most of the settlers at the falls in Vergennes had left when Burgoyne's forces came down the lake in 1777. The only known inhabitants in November, 1778, were Daniel McIntosh, who had been taken prisoner near the lake with Stow and Griswold, and Eli Roberts and his son Durand who lived below the falls. The British forces made camp on the night of November 8 just above the falls.

While the attack on the Otter Creek settlements was in progress, Carleton stayed with his ship to send off several other raiding parties and to bring the fleet back down the lake.

A half hour after the departure of the Otter Creek forces, Carleton sent a smaller detachment ashore four miles farther south to burn Moore's sawmill, which was situated on a small stream seven miles from the lake shore. "They were to go by water untill they got opposite to Putnams Creek, four miles above where I then was," Carleton wrote, "there to land and proceed by a road which lead from thence seven miles back to the Mill."[43]

Moore's mill on the Crown Point Road was not only a supply point for rebel forces, but also the home of one of the most interesting and active of the early settlers, where Whitcomb's scouts and Ethan Allen's Green Mountain Boys often gathered. There was a real possibility that a force of rebels might be assembled there. Carleton's report of extra precautionary measures reflects his awareness of this role of the mill: "I detached Lieut Farquar with thirty men and Cap. Sherwood as a Guide for the purpose of burning Moors Sawmill . . . I sent a Mattross with a Fireball least they should not have time to fire it in the usual way. I ordered Captain Dunlop of 53d with a Subaltern and Thirty men to Support Lt. Farquar with instructions to advance a party half way to the mill for the purpose of reinforceing him if necessary, or facilitating his retreat in case of Accidents."[44]

A total force of sixty men plus their officers was thus sent to burn Moore's mill. By twelve at night Carleton had heard nothing and so concluded that his forces "had met no obstruction."[45]

The next afternoon at two Captain Dunlop caught up with Carleton, who was moving down the lake, and made this report: "That he had gon with Lieut. Farquar himself, that they had proceeded without interuption to a House within five hundred yards of the Mill, that a party of Rebels Posted in this House Fired upon him. He form'd his detatchment and after an engagement of about twenty minnets the Rebel Firing ceas'd intirely. That from their cries he had reason to belive numbers of their Men had been Wounded he drew off his Party and return'd to his Boats with one Man Wounded he concluded that the Party he had met had been the advanced Guard of a detatchment in the Mill and it beeing Night thought it imprudent to Hazard beeing Surrounded in the Woods by Superior numbers."[46]

Vermont reports of attacks on Moore's house and mill are chronologically vague, and it is not entirely clear whether they refer to 1778 or the following year, or to a combination of events in both years. The weather conditions described in them suggest 1779, when a much smaller British force attacked the mill late in November. The sketch of Paul Moore's life and the description of his skill in deceiving and eluding attackers does, however, cast doubts on the British estimates of the size of the force at Moore's house and their guess that a larger number might be waiting at the mill below. The following information is taken from Goodhue's history of Shoreham.[47]

Paul Moore was all his long life a daring adventurer. He was born in Worcester, Massachusetts, in 1731, ran away to sea at the age of twelve, and spent twenty years as a sailor. The story is told that "once the vessel in which he sailed had sprung a leak, and all on board were in peril of their lives, when Moore jumped overboard and stopped the leak by a cake of tallow thrust in at the breach in the planking."[48] He became acquainted with the Vermont area during the French and Indian War, and returned for hunting after the war. In the winter of 1765-1766 he built a hut in Shoreham and lived there completely alone for six months, during which time he caught seventy beavers. He continued hunting and trapping for several years after this and accumulated a modest fortune. One day during

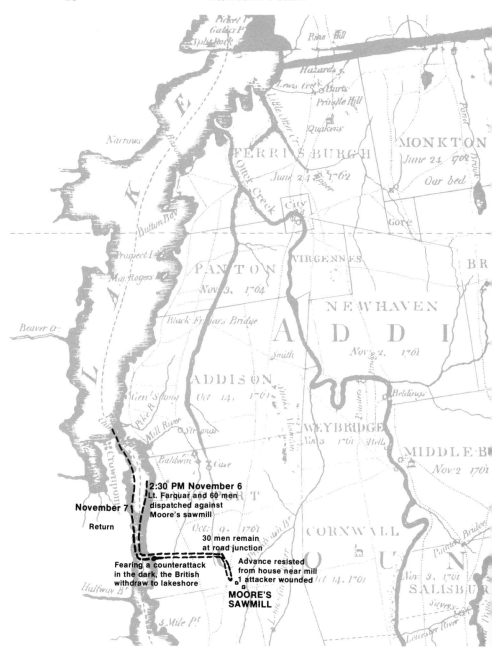

*The Moore's Sawmill Foray/November 6 and 7*

this time he wandered into Fort Ticonderoga and got into an argument with the commander, Colonel Hayes, a dispute which finally led to blows and to a lawsuit. When the question was asked of a witness which struck the other first, he testified that while he "could not tell who struck first, One thing he knew, Mr. Moore struck two blows to Col. Hayes' one."[49]

Moore's house was a meeting place for the Green Mountain Boys during the disputes with New York authorities. After a daring and narrow escape from capture by soldiers near Crown Point in 1772, Ethan Allen and Seth Warner took refuge at Moore's house in Shoreham. Twice during the Revolution Moore himself was taken prisoner by the Indians.

When other inhabitants of the area left for the protection of the forts, Moore and Elijah Kellogg stayed on, sharing a log hut.

*Early the next winter, there were a few soldiers, probably a scouting party, who turned in to spend the night with him. A large party of Indians surrounded the house, which Moore and the men defended. The night was very dark, and while the Indians surrounded the house so as to render escape impossible, Moore slipped outside, and took a side shot at them, by which it was thought two of their number were killed, from traces of blood which appeared upon the ground in the morning. When day light came, a large body of the Indians broke down the door, and rushed into the house. One of the chiefs, whom Moore had known, rushed toward him, as if to kill him. He at once bared his bosom, and looking him in the face, dared him to strike. Another chief interfered, and proposed to burn him. The Indians had previously taken his horse, and had put on the saddle and bridle. Before starting they had a dispute about the ownership of the property, one claiming the horse, another the saddle, and another the bridle. One finally took the horse, and mounted it, with a strip of bark for a bridle; another took the saddle and carried it on his back, and a third person took the bridle in his hand, and set forward on their march, after having set fire to Moore's house, and burnt the saw-mill, and killed his hogs,. The singular appearance of a man riding without a saddle and bridle, and the other two carrying those two articles in triumph, made the old sailor laugh. In this way they proceeded on with the prisoner. Pretending to be more lame than he was, they finally put him on the horse, and the same day they arrived at Crown Point, and encamped for the night. Some of the young men were set to guard him, but as he was lame they did not take the precaution to bind him. Being weary, his guard fell asleep. Moore regarding this as a favorable opportunity to escape, took his gun and blanket, and some*

*Canada biscuit, and set off for the lake, in a direction different from that in which he came, through a thick growth of young saplings, bringing into exercise his sailor habits, making his way for some distance by swinging along from one sapling to another, without touching the ground, until at length he reached the lake. There was at that time snow on the ground, but none on the ice upon the lake. On the shore there was a log reaching out to the ice, he placed himself upon this, and put on his creepers, and walked down the log, and jumped off on the glare ice, leaving no tracks behind him by which he could be traced. After walking far on the ice, he came to one of those cracks which are made by the change of temperature between day and night, being open in the day, and slightly frozen over in the night. Not being able to cross there, he made marks upon the ice with his creepers, and then took them off, and following down the crack, until he had arrived opposite to the marks he had made, as if he had crossed there, and putting on his creepers again he walked off just out of gun shot, and lay down on his blanket as if asleep. When the Indians awoke in the morning, and discovered Moore had escaped, they sent two or three of their number in pursuit. On coming to the crack in the ice where Moore had made the marks, they concluded if he had passed over at that place safely, it would be safe for them to pass. One attempted it and fell in, when Moore with his long gun shot one, and reloaded and shot the other. Having thus disposed of his pursuers, he came to the lake shore in Bridport, so weary that he could go no further. There he concealed himself under a stack of straw, and slept through the night. On awaking the next morning, he was pleased on finding that as it had snowed during the night, no other party could follow his tracks. From thence he proceeded to the place of his former residence, dug out his dried beef from the snow and fled for safety to Brown's camp, which was situated near Miller's bridge in Sudbury, on a high rock nearly perpendicular on the east side, from the base of which issues a large spring. He returned the next season early, and built him a log house.* [50]

While Farquar and Dunlop and their forces were attacking at Moore's mill, another detachment of twenty-four men under Captain Dixon was sent across the lake to destroy Raymond's Mills. The next morning Carleton wrote that he "sett off at day light and moved down the East Side of the Lake destroying the different buildings as I went along but the Wind was so exceeding fresh at N.E. and haveing so few hands in my Boat I proceeded very Slowe."[51] Captain Dixon joined Carleton again at noon and "he reported haveing found a large quantity of Grain and fflour in the different buildings adjoyning to the Mill all of which he effectualy destroyed."[52]

One house that Carleton destroyed in Shoreham was a place where refugees from the March raid in Shelburne were taking refuge. After the earlier attack, Moses Pierson had left his home the next morning and had gone with his family to Shoreham, taking over an unoccupied farm there. An account written by his youngest daughter, Rhoda Pierson Foot, and published in the Burlington Free Press on September 5, 1877, gives these details of the move and the events which followed: "After breakfast they gathered up their things and started on the ice for Shoreham with their horse-teams. The cattle were driven by land thru the woods. There the family made a stop, took a farm, and stayed till fall 78. About this time some scouts from Canada came out and burned up Pierson's house and barn and all the other buildings. They next went to Vergennes where they found a few people whom they took prisoners. After having burned all the log houses, they started for Quebec. Among the prisoners were Mr. Pierson's daughter, Mrs. Sarah Van Arnum, her husband, and a child a year old, named Miles. They had compassion enough for the prisoners to let them ride on the horses they had taken, and, on the way gave back to Mrs. Van Arnum her child's clothing. They were all kept in prison at Quebec till the war was over, when they were exchanged."[53] This family is probably the one listed as "Fananom" in Carleton's List and as "Bennen" in the Canadian records.

That evening (November 7) Carleton could proceed only as far as Buttonmold Bay because of the unfavorable winds. The next morning he sent a scouting party of five Indians "to bring me inteleegence if there was any troops in the Blockhouse at the first Falls on Otter Creek, with directions to examin both Shores as they went up least the Rebels Should be conceald there."[54] While this scouting party was looking over the lower reaches of the creek, Carleton "moved off at Eight halted at the mouth of Creek an hour then proceeded on with the two Gun Boats and the Batteaus."[55] At three the scouting party met them, bringing two prisoners, probably Eli Roberts (Roburds in the Quebec list) and his son Durand. They told Carleton "that there were no Rebel troops in that part of the Country nor had they seen any thing of Captain Ross's Approach."[56]

Carleton proceeded up Otter Creek four miles to the point where it is joined by Dead Creek and there he set up camp and "threw an Abbattis"[57] around it. This camp was not far from the course of Otter Creek above the falls, and Carleton could see the camp fires of

captured cattle
brought here
before shipping

Camp
November 8-10

Scouts - November 8

Raymond's Mills
destroyed November 7

Raiding parties
dispatched - November 6

*The Raymond's Mills Foray/November 8 to November 10*

the force that had gone down the creek: "At 7 I saw Fraser's Fires and Showd them to the Indians who seem'd to doubt it but consented to send a Scout to see, they return'd at 12 had seen Lamott with the Ottawa's Indians who inform'd them that their ffriends were two Miles higher up the Creek."[58]

With the knowledge that Fraser was just above the falls, Carleton's mission was almost completed, and he sent the two gunboats back to Isle aux Noix. Then with the rest of his force he sailed up to the foot of the falls at Vergennes. There he was pleased to learn that "Captain Jones with his twenty Men had been detatched agreeable to my directions to destroy the TownShip of Moncktown which lay Eight Miles back paralel to the Lake. My principal motive for destroying this Township tho' it delay'd me twelve hours was because I knew it to be a remarkable rich one and a Nest of the Greatest Rebels in that part of the Country besides if I could be fortunate enough to Catch Wintress Howick the Indian Interpreter the only person who negociates the Congress business with the Villiages in Canada from thence I should do an esentail Service."[59]

The side expedition to Monkton succeeded up to Carleton's best hopes, and he reported: "At 4 oClock Captain Jones return'd with Several Prisioners of which Howick was one he destroy'd a Considerable Quantity of Arms Amunition Grain Forrage &c and brought off twenty four head of Cattle. I sent the Cattle by land to the mouth of the Creek and moved down with the Detachment in the Boats wee got to our Camp by Eleven oClock."[60]

Monkton was important for the presence of the man called Wintress Howick in Canadian reports. His real name was Winthrop Hoyt; he came from Epping, New Hampshire, and was taken captive during the French and Indian War. During his captivity he spent four years with a Caughnawaga Indian tribe in Canada and was adopted as a son by the chief. Later, Hoyt was one of the Green Mountain Boys, and in the rebellion of the colonies against England, he used his rapport with the Indians to help the cause of independence. In 1777 he was one of a party who took thirteen Tories prisoner at the "Tory Rocks" in the southern part of Monkton, brought them first to Neshobe (Brandon) and then to Ticonderoga.[61] From his base in Monkton, he frequently crossed the northern border into Canada and visited Canadian Indian villages, inciting rebellion among the Indians. Indian attacks were feared by Canadians as much as by their neighbors to the south, and hence the capture of Hoyt was indeed "an essential Service."[62]

Another captive from Monkton was John Bishop, the first settler, who was taken with his sons John, then 21, and Timothy, who was 17. A local history tells that, when the Indians arrived near their home, Mrs. Bishop "repelled the Indians from burning their hay stacks and wheat stacks, knowing them to be her main dependence, by having a kettle of hot water handy and throwing it upon the Indians. They seemed to admire her courage and spared the stacks."[63] This same history reports the capture of another early settler, Ebenezer Stearns, but since his name does not appear on any of the prisoner lists, we can only assume that he either escaped or perished on the way to Isle aux Noix.

The force that attacked Monkton, Captain Jones and his twenty Loyalists, was of a type particularly useful to the British and bitterly hated by the settlers. Made up of former neighbors, such troops had the knowledge of local paths and acquaintance with the habits of the settlers that made them especially sinister attackers. When a group of former inhabitants of an area led a party of Indians to the scattered cabins, there was little chance for even the most remote dwelling or the most hidden clearing to escape notice.

From the mouth of Otter Creek south to beyond Crown Point and Chimney Point, the lake and Otter Creek were now free of rebel buildings and supplies that could help an approaching enemy. Only a short length of sparsely inhabited lakefront remained. Most of the cattle which the Indians had been bringing in from the raided settlements had been transported to Split Rock on the New York side of the lake. Now Carleton ordered that the last group of cattle taken should be added to these and the total numbers checked. He thought that it would amount to between eighty-four and ninety head.[64]

A year later the question of payment for these cattle, which Carleton had promised to the Indians in lieu of scalps, was still unsettled and was a source of tension between the British and the Indians. The Indians claimed that, since eighty head of cattle had been brought safely to Split Rock, they should be paid for eighty head. The British asserted that, since twenty had died on the stormy lake between Split Rock and Isle aux Noix, they had no obligation beyond sixty. A year after the conclusion of the raid, no payment whatsoever had been made, and the Indians were far less cooperative on an expedition made at that time than they had been with Carleton. Clearly not all

British officers took the Indians' claims as seriously as did Carleton, who wrote to British authorities repeatedly in their behalf.

After the cattle had all been ferried past, Carleton "orderd the 31st detatchment to halt twenty four hours at Gililands Creek after the oxon were pass'd by, then to destroy the different Mills and buildings and proceed down the Lake. I orderd the Lee Cutter to cover this detachment. The Maria was orderd to proceed down to Point aufer haveing no further occasion for her."[65]

Carleton himself "with the remainder of the detatchment and the Carleton ran down the East Shore in order to destroy the Buildings &c that wee might find on that side. The Whole moved off at 4 in the Afternoon."[66]

A number of women and children had come in with the men prisoners. For them Carleton "left provis' & a large Rebel Batteau which I had taken, to Carry the Women and Childerin round to Skeansborough."[67] Carleton's charge to the Indians to treat the women and children humanely, and his own orders to send them with provisions down to Skenesborough, where there was a rebel fort, contrast in an interesting manner with the report of Colonel Alexander Webster of the Skenesborough fort to Governor Clinton on November 26, 1778: "I sent of a scout to Crown Point to bring Sure Intilligence of the motions of the Enemy. The Scout was out four days and brought Sure Intilligency that the Enemy was gone off & had burned Six (6) Townships mostly on the Grants. The Men they took prisoners: the women and children they stript, and sent into the Country, Many of them wanting shoes & stockings, among Snow three or four Inches Deep, and only two old men with them, which they did not Choice to take with them—these Miscreants Behaved in this way—the most of the Creaters they Collected into the howses & Sett them on fire and burned them. Others they Cut Large peises out of and Let them run alive. I talked with Several of the women that Escaped. They say they herd them talk much of Skeensborough & it is thought that if we had not been their that they would Certainly a Come."[68]

The "two old men" sent with the women were Elijah Grandey of Panton and Thomas Hinckley, who is reported variously as of Shoreham on the east or of Westport on the west side of the lake, but of whom there appears to be no clear knowledge in either location. Elijah Grandey had come to Vermont from Connecticut about 1773, when he was twenty-five, and was therefore thirty at the time of the raid. He had made a clearing and built a log house in Panton, but the area was still so unsettled that, when he married the sixteen-year-old Salome Smith of Bridport in 1775, they had to go across the lake to Ticonderoga to find someone competent to perform the ceremony. Three years later, every house in Panton was burned except one. Mrs. Grandey "was then but nineteen years of age, but had become accustomed to the visits of the Indians for plunder. After witnessing the burning of her house and furniture, she carried her son Edmund, two years old, to the bateaux at Merrill's Bay, where the women of the vicinity assembled."[69] When Elijah Grandey was released, he took his wife and child to his brother Edmund's in Canaan, Connecticut, and then returned to Vermont to act as a scout and guide until the end of hostilities.

The only house left standing in Panton was that of Timothy Spalding, and the reason why it was spared is not known. Timothy himself escaped out the back of the house as the enemy was approaching the front. Philip and George Spalding of Panton were taken prisoner, but their capture is reported in the Canadian records as on November 4 near Crown Point. Five members of the Holcomb family of Panton, Phineas Holcomb and his sons, Phineas Jr., Joshua, Joseph, and Elisha, and their neighbors Odle (Hordel in the Canadian list) Squire and his son Isley were also reported captured on November 4 and 5 near Crown Point.

Another home destroyed in Panton was that of Peter Ferris on Arnold's Bay. This was the third time in as many years that the Ferris property had suffered in the hostilities on the lake. After Arnold scuttled his fleet in the bay in front of the Ferris property, "his cattle, horses and hogs were shot, and his other property carried off. His orchard trees were cut down, his fences burnt, and nothing left undestroyed, but his house and barn."[70] The next summer, General Burgoyne came up the lake, and a considerable portion of his army camped on the Ferris property. "Two hundred horses were turned into his meadows and grain fields, and they were wholly ruined."[71]

Peter Ferris and his son Squire were active in the service of the American "rebels." In the fall of 1776 they helped Joseph Everest and Phineas Spalding to escape from the British schooner Maria as it lay off Arnold's Bay, and in the following winter Squire Ferris was one of a party who seized two Englishmen near the mouth of Otter Creek and delivered them to General St. Clair at Ticonderoga as spies. In 1778, when Carleton's forces came up Lake Champlain,

Peter and Squire Ferris were deer hunting on the west shore of the lake. There they were seized near the mouth of Putnam's Creek, about six miles south of Crown Point, and carried on board the schooner Maria. Their house and other buildings in Panton were burnt when the raiding forces landed there. One Vermont account reports: "It is said that when Ferris' house was burnt by the British, John Reynolds, a tory from Shoreham, formerly a neighbor of Ferris, in Duchess County, in his zeal for his king, requested the privilege of putting the torch to Ferris' house with his own hands."[72]

As Carleton's forces proceeded slowly north on the lake, they destroyed property and picked up prisoners wherever they could. The local history of Charlotte reports how the first settler of that town, a German named Derick Webb, happened to be captured: "During one of Webb's temporary residences here pending the Revolution he took his children out to Hill's Bay to see the lake, when they were captured by a party of Indians, and Webb was taken to Canada and there detained for several months, while the children were left on the shore. About the same time the Indians visited Mrs. Webb in the cabin, and began to destroy the household effects, preparatory to burning the house. To her entreaties not to burn the cabin they replied that they must set fire to it, as they were under strict orders to do so, but that they would immediately leave, when she might extinguish it if she wished, which she easily succeeded in doing."[73]

From the New York side of the lake, Thomas Hinckley and Benjamin Webster have already been mentioned, Hinckley as one of the men released to take the women and children up the lake to safety, and Webster as a man who helped Benjamin Everest to escape. Two names, John Oaks and James Bodington, appear on the Canadian list of prisoners as taken on November 5 near Crown Point, but they are not to be found in any local history. Except for uncertainty produced by variations in the spelling of names, the other prisoners sent from Carleton to St. John and then the second almost identical list of "Rebel Prisoners brought to Quebec December 6th 1778"[74] can all be located in local histories. In a few cases, when names are the same or similar, it is difficult to be sure of the identity of a prisoner as, for example, whether the Isaac Kellogg of the list is an early settler of Cornwall, where there was a man of that name, or in reality Benjamin Kellogg of Addison, who was taken by Carleton's forces according to early histories of that town.

Carleton's mission was complete with the final checking of the eastern shore of the lake, and he headed back to the Canadian forts. "The fineness of the Night tempted me to proceed. on the 11th about 2 in the morning it Grew so dark and blew so very fresh at S.W. that it seperated the Boats. I put into Grand Isle with 2 more Boats and waited there untill one in the Afternoon. And seeing five Boats I push'd off I got down to Point Aufer by dusk.___Thursday 12th left Pt. Aufer at 10 oClock and reached the Isleand at one. Friday 13th the remainder of the Boats except one came in. that Boat had on Board the Indian presents with a Serjeant and twelve Private of the 29th and a Serjeant and one Private of the 53d Regiment."[75]

Even before Carleton himself reached Isle aux Noix, news of the success of the expedition was on its way to Haldimand. A letter from Powell, dated "November 11th, 1778—3 o'Clock P.M.," reports: "Lieutenant Wild of the 53d Regiment and L. Warburton of the 31st are this moment arrivd with two of the Gun Boats.

"The intelligence they bring is, that Captain Fraser landed at Chimney Point on the 7th Instant with a hundred Regulars and eighty Indians; proceeded thro the Woods to Otter Creek and burnt some houses; brought in Eighty head of Cattle and some disaffected Inhabitants.

"Major Carleton with the rest of his Command moved down the River and took Post at Dead Creek, about five miles up Otter Creek.

"The Houses, Barns, &c, were destroy'd upon both sides of the Lake; a Log house excepted, which was attacked by a Party of our Troops, but being defended by a Superior number of The Rebels, Our People were oblig'd to retire. One Soldier of the 29th Regiment was wounded in that affair.

"The Troops are expected here tomorrow; but as its possible they may be detained by the badness of the weather, I send your Excellency this imperfect account, imagining you are anxious to know the Success of the expedition."[76]

Carleton did arrive on the next day, as this letter from Isle aux Noix, November 14, 1778, shows: "I have the Honr to acquaint your Excellency that I arrived here the 12th with the part of the Detatchment which came down the East shore with me. Those that came down the west shore arrived yesterday, one Boat excepted which had the Indian presents on Board. I fear very much for her as we had uncommon blowing weather & she was very heavy. A Serj't & 14 of the 29th & a Serj't and one Private of the 23d (the 2 last are in

Captn Frasers employ.) on Board. I have taken the liberty to send your Excellency a Copy of my Journall as that will give you a more perfect Idea of the progress of the Detatchment; If I am fortunate enoug to have fulfiled your Intentions I shall esteem my self particularly happy. I doubt not but there will be many applications in behalf of McIntosh but your Excellency may believe me he is a very great Raskale.

"I have not adheard strictly to your Instructions in permitting his wife to come into the Country. Captn Fraser requested it in Compassion to her tho' he Knew the Husband as well as I do. I hope you will not disapprove of it. your Excellency will perceive the names of all the Prisns in the Association list which I send you. 2 families which are come in I sufferd to pass at Captn Sherwoods request, the name of one is Henderson,[77] the others name I have not got but will send it to Captn Le Mainstre as soon as Sherwood arrives. I am not quite convinced that they deserve the Indulgence they have been shown. I think I may venture to say we destroy'd 4 mo Provisn for 12000 men. As we were obliged to destroy a very Considerable quantity of Cattle of all Kinds wich we coud not bring away. I send Lt. Kirkman down with this in case I should have omited any thing in my hurry."[78]

The reaction to this good news was prompt, and on November 19, 1778, Haldimand wrote to Carleton: "Your Letter by Lieutenant Kirkman enclosing a journal of the expedition entrusted to your care, I have received; and cannot but be well pleased with the manner in which you have executed my orders, and beg you will as well As the Officers And Men under your command accept of my thanks for the good conduct, vigilance and activity shown upon the occasion, which redounds much to their credit, And is very satisfactory to me. Whenever you have leisure I shall be glad to have from you, for my own satisfaction, As particular a detail as you can give of every place you went to enumerating as much as possible every thing you destroyed, and the local description of every tenement you burned. With every intelligence you have received of the situation of the Rebells, their Magazines or Stores, in the interior parts from whence you went to. The agreement you made with the savages respecting the Cattle, you have my approbation to fulfill."[79]

The list of things destroyed and two sketches of Otter Creek, its mouth and the falls at Vergennes, were not sent until January, after a reminder from Haldimand's secretary. Meanwhile, however, two

personnel matters arising out of the raid were discussed in letters.
On November 24, 1778, Carleton reported to Haldimand that some
of the Indians on the raid had been badly managed by the British
officers in charge of them:

*I take the liberty of troubling your Excellency relative to the Indians of the
Lake of Two Mountains. In the course of my Expedition I found those
Indians much alterd for the worse from what I had know them for several
years. I spoke to some of the most sensible & leading men among the Chiefs, &
from their Answers cou'd see they were led a stray by two low fellows who live
with them and having the Advantage of speaking their language persuades
them to all sorts of irregularities & wrong headedness. If your Excellency
thougt it proper to order An Officer to be appointed who from time to time can
go and see them, it wou'd gradually wean them from the influence of those
people & bring them to what they certainly were, the best and most loyal
subjects you had at the worst of tiems.*

*As your Excellency was pleased to say you'd employ Mr. Brown in that
department I gave him the Command of the Canasatagua's for the Expedition
& introduced him to the Chiefs as a young officer under whome they were
probably to serve, they were very much pleased at it, and as it will be the latter
end of Decr before there will be sufficient snow for scouting any distance if
you order'd Lt Brown over there for that time it wou'd be Commincing an
acquaintance which he might renew from time to time untill his duty here
permited his constant residence there. I took great pains to shew them their
folly before they left this but it requires more patience to conduct Indians than
most Genln are possest of. I have order'd Lt Brown to Montreal to wait your
commands.* [80]

The second problem was with a white officer, Captain Ross, who
commanded the party raiding the Gillilands Creek area on the west
side of the Lake. Carleton's letter to Brigadier General Powell ex-
plains the incident: "I am sorry to find that Captn. Ross thinks his
character is likely to suffer so materealy in consequence of my
having reported to you that it was owing to his not understandg my
orders properly, The Buildings on Gillilands Creek were not destroy'd. I have only to say I am confident it was my intentions to have
order'd it, but as Captn. Ross is so very clear that He never did
receive any such orders, I can only suppose that in the Hurry I must
have forgot to mention that part of my Instructions to Him."[81]

Haldimand was delighted with the results of the expedition. Not
only do his letters to Carleton reflect this, but he also reported the

success of the raid in glowing terms to Lord Germain in England. As late as the following March, he continued to refer to the raid and its effects: "The Rebels continue to threaten invading the Province, but the Destruction of the Cattle, Forage &c upon Otter Creek and the Edge of the Lake Last Fall, would alone have greatly increased the difficulty of their approach. And as Lake Champlain begins to break up I think any attempt that way impracticable for the remainder of the winter."[82]

The military expedition was, in the Canadian view, a signal success. However, the Indians were clamoring for payment for the cattle they had brought in. They had been promised eight dollars apiece for oxen, and, as their part of the bargain, they had not taken the scalps which were a status symbol in their society. By January they were asking to be sent back along Otter Creek for scalps. Powell wrote to Haldimand on January 17, 1779, "I have receiv'd a letter from Major Carleton mentioning that the Indians have demanded to be sent to Otter Creek to take some scalps. I have desir'd him not to permit them to go 'till your pleasure is known."[83] Haldimand wrote to Carleton on January 21, 1779, "If the Indians you have should be inclined to go out I shall have no objections provided it be to procure intelligence and that they proceed to no greater length than taking prisoners, but you must insist upon their containing themselves within the bounds of humanity towards them, otherwise they must not be suffered to go."[84]

Thirty-nine "disaffected Inhabitants"[85] are mentioned in a letter of November 15, 1778, from Powell to Haldimand. These prisoners arrived in Quebec on December 6, 1778.

"When any of those prisoners undertake to make their escape from this place they show more ingenuity to effect it than I had any apprehention of."

JOHN NAIRNE

# 5

## The
## Prisoners

THE PRISONERS from Carleton's raid joined others who had been taken earlier. More were added later, especially in the fall of 1779, when another smaller raid touched Lake Champlain and the part of Otter Creek between Middlebury and Pittsford. When an exchange of prisoners was arranged in 1782, forty-eight Vermont prisoners held by the Canadians were released in exchange for British prisoners held in Vermont.

Early histories report that "the vessels proceeded with their prisoners to St. Johns; from thence they were marched to Sorel, and it was the intention of the captors to have continued their march down the St. Lawrence to Quebec. At Sorel they crossed the St. Lawrence, and soon after a heavy snow storm came on, which making it impossible to continue the march, trains were seized in all directions, and on these they were driven to Quebec."[1] "The prisoners, on their arrival at Quebec, were for a time kept on board a prison ship; but were afterwards removed to a prison on land."[2]

After the prisoners were taken from the prison ship to the prison in Quebec, they lost no time in beginning attempts to escape. The chronology of the escapes is not altogether clear from the local histories where they are recorded, and the accounts are in minor details contradictory. In sum, however, they provide a picture of men determined to get back to homes and families, of their encounters with friendly and unfriendly citizens, and often of recapture and re-escape.

After the first escape attempt, in which some of the prisoners dug under the walls, "they were divided, and about one hundred of them were sent down the river one hundred miles and employed in getting out timber for building barracks."[3]

On April 13, 1779, the colonists taken in Carleton's raid petitioned to be allowed to return to their families. The petition, written by Peter Ferris, reads:

"May yt plaese Your Excellency

"We Your Excellency's most humble petitioners beg leave to lay before your Excellency this our humble petition hoping to have both a gracious hearing and answer.

"By your Excellency's orders we the inhabitants of the Grants near Crown-point was In the month of November last taken our houses plunder burnt and provisions destroyd by savages and we marched here prisoners nor any reason given or complaint made wherein we had offended. we having during the present unhappy contest had from time to time his Majesty's general officer's orders to stay peacibly on our several plantations and their promises that we should not be molested.

"Confiding in this we was embolden to stay and enjoy our living hoping that our conduct would be such as would merritted your Excellency's permission for a continuance of the same favours.

"And since it has not, we in the most pathetic manner most humbly ask your Excellency to take into Consideration our Necessitous condition in Regard of our unhappy families which is cast on the mercy of the contry, their living destroyd. We are more sollicitous as the Spring is far advancd and call upon by the strongest ties of Nature both of consanguinity and affinity.

"We therefore humbly ask that in the first convenient opitunity most consistent with your good will and pleasure we may be sent in quest of our destrest and sufring families the unhappy road we come which would be favour as greatfully acknowledged as yt is beneficial and acceptable to your most humble servants.

                                        Peter Ferish
        In Provost April 13th 1779
                        Phineas Hollcomb
                                in behalf of the others"[4]

The petition was addressed to "His Excellency General Haldimond Capt. Gen Govr and Comander in Cheif in & over His Majesty's Province of Canada."

The petition does not appear to have been heeded by the gover-

nor, since the only prisoners who returned before 1782 were those
who managed to escape and make their way back through the
wilderness. Among the escapees was Thomas Sanford of Weybridge. A letter written by him to his wife, who was then in Rutland, is
preserved among the Canadian papers. It is dated March 15 (probably 1780, since his escape is reported in May of that year) and was
evidently intercepted by the British. It reads:

> "loven wif
>
> "I imbras this opertunety to writ this few line to let you no I ham in
> good helth at present blesed God for hit hopen this few lins wil find
> you in the same. I hav hard from you sence I hav bin in prison and
> ham glad to her you and Childer are in helth. think not long of
> absens tis the forton of war and the hand of the Lord of hosts that
> dos hit. I hav try too tims to run to you and my cuntry but was cach and
> ham now so clos confin tis imposibal if the berer get thro wil tel you
> hal abot hit. how we brib Centry to cary leter to god frind in the toun
> to provid al necesry for go hof, and too soger good whigs to go along
> — use them wel and tel al loven frinds to liberty the sam. too
> desarted latly. did my best to go long but wod not do hope the got saf
> thro the hands of the sarpents. wil try agen if tim promits, ham wel
> hof for vitels and mony Comesary is god Man dos not let hus want
> for nothen — ham now writen in the dark — god presarve you my
> dear and loven wif til deth —
>
> Thos. Sanford
>
> Mr. Smith be plase send this leter to my wif."[5]

The letter is addressed to "Mrs. Sanford, Car Mr. Smith at Rutland,"
but since it is among the Canadian papers it evidently did not get
through to her.

In May, 1780, two letters from Major John Nairne, in charge of
prisoners cutting timber at Malbay, report escapes. On May 14,
1780, he wrote: "It gives me great concern to Acquaint you, and to
beg that you would inform His Excellency that notwithstanding
every precaution that we imagined was taken to secure her, the
Rebel prisoners, Eight of them, last night, found the means, to get
the Batteau and have made off...I am really ashamed...Their
names are:

| | |
|---|---|
| Peter Ferris, aged about | 55 years |
| Squire Ferris | 16 |
| Claudius Brittle | 44 |
| Claudius Brittle | 18 |

| Nathan Smith | 28 |
| Marshall Smith | 23 |
| Justus Sturtevant | 42 |
| John Ward | 21 |

They are all rather tall."[6]

This account is given by Samuel Swift of the escape of Nathan and Marshall Smith and John Ward:

*In the spring of 1780, after two dreary winters, in which several of the party died, the prisoners had liberty to remove thirty leagues down the River St. Lawrence, to work. About forty went, among whom were the two Smiths and Ward. They landed the first of May, on the south\* side, where the river was twenty-seven miles wide. In the night of the 13th, eight of the prisoners took a batteau and crossed the river and landed in a perfect wilderness. They here separated into two parties, Justus Sturdevant, of Weybridge joining the three Bridport men. They traveled by night, and when in the neighborhood of settlements, secreted themselves by day. They occasionally met Frenchmen, who appeared friendly; but on the 20th, when nearly opposite Quebec, they called on two Frenchmen for aid in crossing a swollen river. One of them stated that he was an officer, and dared not let them pass. He seized his gun and declared them prisoners. The other took up an axe, and both stood against the door to prevent their escape. Nathan Smith said to his comrades, 'we must go,' and seized the man with the gun, and the other prisoners laid hold of the other Frenchman, and they thrust them aside, and all escaped except Sturdevant, who remained a prisoner until the close of the war. Some days after, four Indians, armed with guns and knives, came upon them, but they sprang into the woods and escaped, and traveled all night until noon the next day, when being not far from Three Rivers, they lay down and slept. But soon each was awakened by an Indian having fast hold of him. They were committed to prison at Three Rivers. Three sides of the prison were of stone, the other of wood. After being in prison three weeks, they began to cut into the wooden wall with a jack-knife, and in a week had cut through it sufficiently to escape into an adjoining room. Having drawn a week's provisions, they cut up their bed clothes, and let themselves down, so near the window of the room below, that they saw the officers there assembled, and were not more than a rod from the sentinel in his box. Thence they continued to travel by night, and lay by in the day time. To supply themselves with food, they took a lamb in one place and a turkey and other fowls in others. They kept off from the river to avoid the*

---

\* Accurately quoted but must be *north* according to geography and subsequent events.

*Indians, who they learned were in pursuit of them, and had been offered a
bounty for their apprehension. They at length crossed the St. Lawrence and
traveled to the River Sorel, and thence through the wilderness, with incredible
hardships and suffering, having killed an ox on the way for thier sustenance,
and at length arrived at the house of Asa Hemenway, in Bridport, which
alone had survived the desolations of the war. The next day they reached the
picket fort at Pittsford. From the time of their escape, ninety miles below
Quebec, including their imprisonment, they had not changed their clothes,
and had few left to be changed.* [7]

Abby Hemenway's account agrees in essentials with Swift's, but
adds a few details: "Three of them again made their escape that
night—Ward and the two Smiths— and after being again taken by
the Indians, and again escaping, pursued by the Indians fourteen
days and nights, all their knowledge of the Indian craft and devices
being put to the utmost trial, they finally succeeded in throwing off
their pursuers and arrived in Panton, where they met three Ameri-
cans, on a scout, from whom they got provisions; which was the first
food they had tasted since their last escape, except such as they
procured in the woods—in all, twenty days. The next day they
stopped at Hemenway's, in Bridport. (Hemenway never left his farm
through all the war.) After one day's rest, they pushed on to
Pittsford."[8]

Peter Ferris and his son Squire, who had suffered so much at the
hands of British forces on the lake, were imprisoned with the other
captives at Quebec.

*Soon after,* reads an account written by Philip C. Tucker, who had the
facts from Squire Ferris himself, *some of them having contrived to escape,
they were divided, and about one hundred of them were sent down the river
one hundred miles and employed in getting out timber for building barracks.
Mr. Ferris and his son were sent among this number in the month of January,
1779. In the spring following nine of the prisoners, among whom were Mr.
Ferris and his son, seized a batteau in the night, in which they crossed to the
east side of the river, where it was fifteen miles wide. On landing they set the
batteau adrift, separated into two parties, and made the best of their way up
the river. They had brought provisions with them, and avoiding the settlements, and traveling only in the night, the party, with which the two Ferrises
remained, arrived opposite the Three Rivers on the fourth day. They crossed
in the night, but were discovered and retaken. The remainder of the party did*

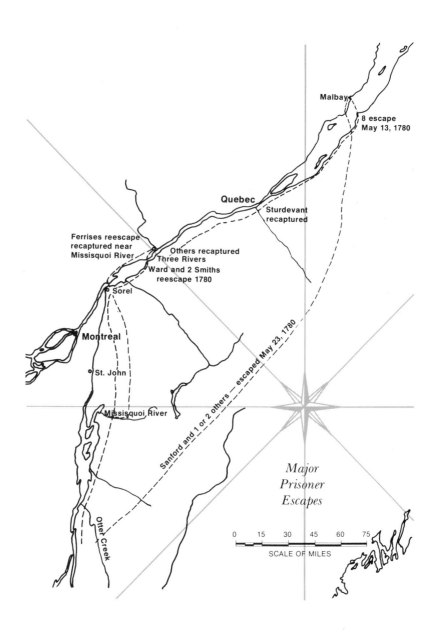

Malbay

8 escape
May 13, 1780

Quebec

Sturdevant
recaptured

Ferrises reescape
recaptured near
Missisquoi River

Others recaptured
Three Rivers
Ward and 2 Smiths
reescape 1780

Sorel

Montreal

St. John

Missisquoi River

Sanford and 1 or 2 others — escaped May 23, 1780

Otter Creek

*Major
Prisoner
Escapes*

0    15    30    45    60    75

SCALE OF MILES

not get so far, having been retaken by a body of Indians in the neighborhood of Quebec. The party of the Ferrises were put into jail at Three Rivers, where they remained eighteen months. During this time they made one attempt to escape, but were discovered and were then placed in a dungeon for seventy-two days. At this time the father and son were separated.

Squire Ferris, the son, describes the dungeon where he was confined, as an apartment eight feet by ten, and so low that he could not stand up in it, and that the one occupied by his father adjoined it, and was of the same character. The only light was admitted by a small hole about eight by ten inches in size, which was crossed by iron grates. The hole which admitted this light was level with the ground, and the water from the eaves of the jail poured through it into the dungeon, whenever it rained. The straw given them to sleep on was frequently wet in this way, and the confined air, dampness and filth, not to be avoided, made their sufferings of the severest kind. While they were confined here, another place was prepared for them, to which they were transferred after the dungeon suffering of seventy-two days. This place was opposite the guard room, and upon being removed to it, they were told, 'you damned rebels, you can't get out of this.' Here the father and son were again put together in the same room. The place was not however so impregnable as was supposed, for in about six weeks the prisoners made an excavation under the wall, in the night, and made their escape. There were six prisoners in the room at this time. Upon escaping, the parties separated, Mr. Ferris and his son remaining together. They went up the river nearly opposite Sorel, where, two days afterward, they crossed the St. Lawrence in a canoe, and took to the woods. Their design was to reach New Hampshire, but having lost their way in the woods they struck Missique River, down which they went for a few miles, and were again retaken by a British guard, who were with a party getting out timber, and by them were carried again prisoners to St. Johns. They were taken twenty-one days after their escape, and had been nineteen days in the woods, during all which time they had only a four pound loaf of wheat bread, one pound of salt beef and some tea for food. They made their tea in a tin quart cup, and produced fire by a flint and the blade of a jack-knife. For four days before they were retaken, they had nothing for food but tea, and were so weak they could barely walk. The forces at St. Johns were then commanded by Col. St. Leger, a brutal drunkard, who ordered the prisoners to be ironed together, and put them in a dungeon for fourteen days. At the end of which time, and ironed hand in hand to each other, they were sent to Chamblee, and from there by the rivers Sorel and St. Lawrence to Quebec. At Quebec they were returned to their old prison, in which they remained until June, 1782, when they were brought from thence to Whitehall and there exchanged for British prisoners.

*From their capture to their exchange was three years and eight months.* [9]

On May 26, 1780, Major Nairne wrote

*to report that Six more of the Rebel prisoners have made their escape from this place /viz./ four of them in the night of the 17th they took a Birch Canoo out of a Barn where it was Concealed under Straw, with which they went along till at a man's house about three Lagues from this place finding a small Boat in which they were seen next morning crossing the River St. Lawrence towards the Parish of Camarasbia. The other two disappeared the 23d Inst. and I have not yet had any account which way they have gone. Every Boat and Canoo, is secured in the best manner the people are able, but when any of those prisoners undertake to make their escape from this place they show more ingenuity to effect it than I had any apprehention of. They receive their provisions dayly so that last Six who deserted had none along with them. It's to be supposed that they depend upon receiving assistance from the Country people, and if the Country people will not Stop them or give any information of them, those only will remain here who do not Choose to make an attemp to escape. The prisoners who are here at present, being thirteen in number, put on the appearance of most innocent people and pretend that they will not follow the bad example of the others, but say that they wish much to be exchanged and to get home to their own Country. I would be glad to know the Generals intentions now with regard to building Barracks here, because should there be no more prisoners sent to this place the few that remain may be lodged in a Small Building. Canadien workmen must now be employed for that purpose, which will be expensive as only two old men of the prisoners understand anything of Carpenter work. I put a Stop to working at those Barracks since the eight men deserted till I hear from His Excellency on this subject. Should the Barracks not be erected here, the timber that's prepared for them might be carried elsewhere . . .The names of the Six Deserters are Bengimin Pain, Benagen Webster, Thom. Sandford, John Ellis, Michel Lighthall, Andrew Sherward.* [10]

From Swift's history of Addison County comes this account of Thomas Sanford's escape: "They dug through the walls of the prison and escaped, but were retaken and recommitted, except Thomas Sanford and one or two others from Vermont, who after wandering a long time through the wilderness of New Hampshire and Maine reached their families . . .When Mr. Sanford was captured he had two horses and a colt which were left behind without any one to take care of them. He returned, as related above, after three years absence, expecting to find his horses dead. But he found them alive, except the colt, which the Indians shot. They had lived on the Beaver Meadows, in the neighborhood, and were found some distance from where Sanford left them. They had become very wild; but Sanford had given each of them a name, and when he called them by their names they came to him and were easily taken, they recognizing either their names or their master's voice."[11]

The use of Vermont prisoners to help build barracks down the St. Lawrence River led to repeated escape attempts. A year after Sanford's successful escape, two others taken by Carleton, Winthrop Hoyt of Monkton and Ezra Squires of Panton, escaped in 1781 but were retaken at the St. Francis River.[12]

While Sanford did succeed in escaping, his nearest neighbor in Weybridge, Claudius Brittell, was still a prisoner in 1782, as this petition dated September, 1782 shows:

"To His Excellency Frederick Haldimand Esqr Governor & Commander in Chief in and over the Province of Quebec &c

"The Memorial of Claudius Britaill In Behalf of himself And Son Humbly Sheweth

"That Whereas Your Memorialist with his son were made Prisoners by Capt. Fraser of the 34th Regt. on the 8 Day of November 1778 it being the same Expedition Commanded by Major Carleton As we were at our own home And at our Lawfull Calling At a place called Waybridge, on Otter Creek, in the State of Vermont. We being Put into Prison at Quebec for the Space of Fourteen Months At the End of which Term Myself And Son Took the Oath of Alleigance At the same time were permitted to work in the Province. All which we hear Most Strictly Adhered to

"Now if your Excellency will be Graciously Pleas'd to Grant to his Memorialist a Pass to Return to the said Otter Creek with his Son, I the said Memorialist both hereby Promise and Engadge that I will At all times behave Myself as a faithfull Subject, and that I nor My Son will never do Anything that shall be either Detrimental or offencive to his Majestys Service, but in All things And at all times will Demean Myself As a faithfull Subject

"And as in Duty Bound Shall ever Pray

Claudius Bretell

St Johns 15 September 1782

NB. As my wife and Child is Lately Come to St. Johns I Pray his Excelency will Just Mention her in the Passport for her to Return With me.[13]

The wording and spelling of this document are in such contrast to the other two prisoners' papers which have been preserved that it appears to have been written by an official clerk. By the time Brittell's appeal was made, most of the Vermonters had returned home, and his and his son's return was evidently delayed by their going over to the Canadian side.

Vermont documents give a varied picture of the fate of the prisoners. Several died in prison, including David Stow on December 31, 1778, Benjamin Kellogg during the same winter, and Joshua and Samuel Holcomb during the summer of 1781. The Holcomb brothers' father, who had escaped, died in September of that same year in Rutland.

Clark Stow, whose father died in prison, was only fifteen when he was taken prisoner. He "was selected by a French lady, and employed by her as a house servant, until he, with the rest, was exchanged and released in 1782. After his release in October he went to Great Barrington, Mass., to which the family had removed, and in March, 1783, they returned to Weybridge."[14]

The two younger Holcomb boys, Joseph and Elisha, were also only 16 and 15 when taken prisoner. They, "allowed more liberty, and treated with less severity (being permitted to aid in the care of the sick prisoners), escaped the disease and death which was the sad fate of so many of their companions in misery, and were exchanged after three years and eight months imprisonment."[15]

John Bishop of Monkton found in his imprisonment a basis for a new life. In the words of the local history:

*It appears that during his captivity, his uniform good conduct obliging behavior, so far won the good will of those in charge of the prison, that as a mark of approbation and particular favor he was granted access to books and was assisted in the study of mathematics for which he had a decided taste. Naturally gifted with perceptions and a retentative memory, and being with all of an observant and inquiring nature, he readily saw that in patiently resigning himself to the situation he was in, and by improving his powers and opportunities to the utmost of his ability, he would be fitting himself to meet any emergency that might arise once he was liberated. By these means he acquired a knowledge of the science of surveying, which after his return home, (to Monkton), was turned to practical account. He followed this profession several years here, finally deciding to return to Canada with the idea of promoting another*

*settlement and the taking up of land which he had found to his liking . . .
having formed valuable acquaintances with parties of Quebec, during his
compulsory sojourn in that City, this time voluntarily, and was highly favored
on meeting with friends who were able and willing to forward his wishes and
plans. He had no doubt while back here in Monkton, talked with several of the
families in the community and received the assurance that they would be
interested in the venture if they were to be included in the proprietorship in a
new township in Canada . . . He therefor took the preliminary steps toward
obtaining for himself and associates the grant of a township of land. Next he
visited the tract designated, made some necessary preparation for the removal
there, and returned to Vermont. In October, 1800, he brought his wife and
seven children, these all under fifteen years of age, to the new home provided
for them in the wilderness of Dudswell.*

*A widowed sister named Chaffee, and her son accompanied the family, these
being the first permanent residents of the tract of land settled on . . . Owing to
the wretched state of the roads, their wagon was left at Derby, Vermont, and
the remainder of the journey was made on horseback through ways almost
impassable due to the muddy conditions, until they reached what was called
the Little Forks. Here there were a few Log Dwellings, and from this point, the
line was indicated by marks on the trees alone. Their progress was necessarily
slow, eight or ten miles being considered quite a day's accomplishment for this
manner of traveling. Several associates of families came to the tract of
ground soon after this . . . The business connected with the settlement of which
he was the head and founder, required Mr. Bishop to be frequently away from
home, during which journeys he was a sufferer of fatigue and exposure. On
one of these trips made in the month of March, he was taken sick and lay ill at
the house of a friend about 14 miles from home, until the following June,
when, anxious as he said, to reach his home to die, he was carefully conveyed to
the river, at Fort Francis, and brought in an Indian bark canoe to within a
short distance of the home, there making the rest of the journey on land. After
reaching his home, he never again ventured away, altho he lived until August
of that year.* [16]

Not all the prisoners cooperated with their captors as well as John
Bishop. Local history reports of Eli Roberts and his son Durand,
who were taken near the Vergennes falls, that "while prisoners they
were sent under guard to labor, but that Eli refused to work for the
British, and was so free in his remarks on the subject that he was not
allowed to leave as soon as his son."[17]

Another prisoner who was detained longer than the others was
Winthrop Hoyt, the Indian interpreter captured in Monkton. In
May, 1782, he is mentioned in a Canadian letter as "being among the
number of prisoners asked for last year by Vermont."[18]When the
Canadian authorities realized that Hoyt was among those being sent
back, however, they blocked his release. The order to separate Hoyt
from the others came from the Commander-in-Chief, who wanted
the matter handled discreetly, as this letter from his aid shows: "His
Excellency the Commander-in-Chief finding that one Withrop Hoit
is among the Vermont prisoners for exchange under your care, he is
pleased to direct that you will deliver him up to the officer commanding at Three Rivers as it is not intended he shall be exchanged.
He is an Indian interpreter, has much influence with that people,
and is a violent rebel, however that no unfavorable report may be
made by those who return, the general desires he may be separated
from them without any appearance of severity, and just told that he
cannot be exchanged this opportunity. You will nevertheless take
particular care that he is safe delivered into the custody at Three
Rivers."[19] Other letters mention returning Hoyt "on pretense of his
receiving some instructions" [20] and say that he is to be "put in
irons"[21] and that "care must be taken that the Vermont prisoners do
not perceive that any treatment, the least harsh is shewn to
Him—No Indians or indeed any other persons must be permitted to
see him."[22] In March 1783, the Vermont records show "expenses
paid out with a flag to Canada . . .to recover Withrop Hoit and John
and Henry Lovel, prisoners in close confinement at Quebec."[23]

After being released, Winthrop Hoyt set out for home, but before
he reached there he learned that his wife, thinking him dead, had
married a Mr. Allen. When he received this information, he turned
back without going to see her and returned to Canada, where he
married another woman. He settled in northern Vermont and is
listed in the 1790 census of St. Albans, and in 1810 and 1813 in
Swanton. It is reported that Nathan Hoyt, Winthrop's son by his first
marriage, visited Winthrop in his new home and found there several
young half brothers.[24]

Philip and George Spalding are reported to have tried with mixed
success to escape: "Philip, with some others, wandered in the woods
21 days, when they struck the Connecticut River, at the great Ox-
bow, in Newbury. George was retaken and put in irons, but afterwards offered his liberty if he would first go one trip in a vessel to

Great Britain. Stopping at some port in Ireland, he availed himself of his permission to go ashore with the crew, when he was taken by a press-gang, and nothing more is known of him. Philip, after his return, enlisted and served through the war."[25]

John Griswold also apparently disappeared in Ireland. According to information supplied by his brothers, "John Griswold Jun. enlisted on board a British vessel at Quebec, upon a promise, that he should be restored to his liberty, on the arrival of the vessel in Ireland. He was never heard of afterward."[26]

Two other prisoners taken on the shores of Lake Champlain a year after Carleton's raid participated in escape attempts and played a major role in the release and exchange of prisoners. Benjamin Stevens of Cornwall "was captured with three others, in a boat on Lake Champlain, near Split Rock, in Charlotte, in May, 1779. Being pursued by the Tories and Indians from the shore, and one of the men, Jonathan Rowley, being killed by a shot from the pursuers, they surrendered. Stevens was then seventeen years old and resided in Rutland County...The prisoners were taken to Chamblee, 'thrust into a small prison, ironed two together and fed for nine days on no other food than dry peas uncooked. From thence they were taken to Quebec, where Mr. Stevens spent three New Year's days in one room.' Twice they made their escape, and after traveling a long time in a destitute and suffering condition, at one time in the dead of winter, and a part of the time living on roots and the bark of trees, until one of the party died, they were retaken and recommitted, and in June, 1782, were exchanged at Whitehall."[27]

The other prisoner was Paul Moore, whose mill had been the target of an attack by Carleton's forces. The account of his captivity reads:

*Some time in the year 1780, as nearly as can now be ascertained, Mr. Moore went on business to the Scotch settlement, at the outlet of Lake George, where he was taken by a band of Tories and Indians. He was told by them that his head would be a button for a halter, because he had killed the Indians who were sent after him the year before. He was taken by them to Quebec, and held a prisoner for about six months. While there he learned of the Squaws to make baskets. He sold his rations to them, and got them to sell his baskets, by which means he purchased milk and such other food as he could eat. While there he wrote a letter to the provincial Governor, requesting new straw and more blankets for himself and the other prisoners, who were suffering. The Governor sent him an unkind answer, accusing him of impudence. A second letter of Moore, in terms still more decided and bold, induced the Governor to send the straw and blankets.*

*During his captivity, Mr. Moore wrote a letter to Gov. Chittenden, giving an account of the suffering condition of the prisoners. This, with an application of their friends, induced the Governor to send a flag, with a letter to the commanding officer in Canada, requesting their release or exchange. A favorable answer was returned by Gen. Haldimand, who came up Lake Champlain with great force, and sent a flag at the same time to Ethan Allen, proposing a cessation of hostilities with Vermont, during the negotiation for the exchange of prisoners. This proposal was acceded to by Allen, on condition that the adjacent territory of New York should be included. Early in 1781, Ira Allen was appointed to settle a cartel with the British for an exchange of prisoners. This was effected, and Moore and his fellow prisoners were released, and an arrangement was entered into between the authorities of Vermont and Canada, by which hostilities ceased to a very great extent, and an army of ten thousand men in Canada was kept in a state of inactivity for the space of nearly three years. If that force had been sent forward to co-operate with the British army in New York, the result of the effort to establish American Independence might have failed entirely, or have been delayed to a longer period . . .*

*On his return from captivity, it is said that he revisited the place of his former residence, and in taking a survey of the desolations around him, as he walked up back from his former dwelling he fixed his eye on a singular looking object, which upon more careful observation he found to be a colt, which being very poor, presented a nondescript appearance, its hair shaggy, and lying in every direction; and at a little distance from the colt, what should he see, but his old pet mare. He called her by her name, and as soon as she heard the old familiar voice, she ran to her master, and laid her head on his shoulder as if she would most fondly embrace him, who was dead but now alive. This affected him to tears. The old favorite beast, that he thought had perished, had not only supported herself by pawing through the snow for grass, but had sustained the life of the strange looking colt, which was seen by her side.* [28]

In 1782 most of the prisoners were released to find their way back to their families. 1783 saw them returning to their burned out cabins, ruined orchards, and trampled fields to start again to build a life in the wilderness. The description of what settlers in New Haven found is typical of conditions throughout the area: "Their farms, which had been partially cleared, remained waste during their absence, and were covered with a thick growth of bushes. A portion of the live stock that escaped slaughter or capture by the enemy, ranged in the woods, grazing in summer, and browsing in winter, and were found at the return of the settlers, to have multiplied, rather than diminished. They had formed a trail from the clearings on the creek to a beaver meadow or prairie of nearly 100 acres, covered with wild grass, and situated between Beach and Town hill. It is related that one of the settlers was at work in the field, having with him a yoke of oxen fastened by a chain to a tree. When the alarm was given of the approach of the enemy, in his haste to release the cattle, and drive them to a place of security, he unhitched the chain from the yoke, leaving it wound around the body of the tree. The tree, in its growth, finally covered the chain, and it remained undiscovered until many years afterwards, when the tree was cut down."[29]

Life went on, and the families who had been uprooted in Carleton's raid returned and put down new roots. They had been active and adventurous pioneers when they first came to Vermont, and they continued to be vigorous citizens in the fourteenth state of the new nation. Their names appear among the officers of town governments, as respected members of church groups, and on volunteer militia rolls.

Vermont is proud to claim their descendants among its citizens today.

# Appendices

# Appendices

# NOTES

Public Archives of Canada, the source of many of the documents, will be noted as PAC.

## Introduction

1 Haldimand to Carleton, October 17, 1778 (trans. from French) (PAC)
2 *Ibid.*
3 Carleton's Journal (PAC)
4 Petition of Peter Ferris, April 13, 1779 (PAC)
5 Haldimand to Germain, October 15, 1778 (PAC)

## Chapter 1. The Canadian Situation

1 Haldimand to Germain, July 25, 1778 (PAC)
2 *Records of the Council of Safety and Governor and Council of the State of Vermont* (Montpelier, Vt.: published by the State, 1873), I, p. 217
3 Haldimand to Germain, October 18, 1778 (PAC)
4 Quoted in Jean N. McIlwraith, *Sir Frederick Haldimand*, (Toronto: Morang & Co.; 1910), pp. 208-210
5 Haldimand to Germain, July 28, 1778 (PAC)
6 Haldimand to Peters, July 25, 1778 (PAC)
7 Peters to Haldimand, August 11, 1778 (PAC)
8 Haldimand to Germain, October 15, 1778 (PAC)

## Chapter 2. Preparations

1 *Letters of Brunswick and Hessian Officers during the American Revolution*, trans. by William L. Stone (assisted by August Hund), (Albany, N.Y.: J. Munsell's Sons, 1891), p. 64
2 Howard H. Peckham, *The War for Independence. A Military History* (Chicago, Ill: University of Chicago Press, 1958), p. 61
3 *Brunswick and Hessian letters.* pp. 64-65
4 A.G. Bradley, *Lord Dorchester* (London: T.C. and E.C. Jack; and Toronto, Morang and Co., Ltd., 1907), pp. 75-76
5 Twiss to Haldimand, July 27, 1778 (PAC)
6 Powell to Haldimand, September 30, 1778 (PAC)
7 Powell to Haldimand, October 24, 1778 (PAC)
8 Powell to Haldimand, October 28, 1778 (PAC)
9 Frazer to Haldimand, October 19, 1778 (PAC)
10 Haldimand to Powell, October 17, 1778 (PAC)
11 Haldimand to Chambers, October 17, 1778 (PAC)
12 F.L.M. to Macbean, October 17, 1778 (PAC)
13 Haldimand to Powell, October 19, 1778 (PAC)
14 Powell to Haldimand, September 17, 1778 (PAC)
15 Powell to Haldimand, October 24, 1778 (PAC)
16. *Ibid.*
17 *Ibid.*
18 *Ibid.*

# Carleton's Raid

## Chapter 3. Situation in the Champlain Valley

1 Samuel Swift, *History of the Town of Middlebury in the County of Addison, Vermont,* to which is Prefixed a Statistical and Historical Account of the County (Rutland: Charles E. Tuttle Company, 1971: reprint of first edition, Middlebury, Vermont: A.H. Copeland, 1856), p. 69
2 Hiland Hall, *The History of Vermont from its Discovery to its Admission into the Union in 1791* (Albany, N.Y.: Joel Munsell, 1868), pp. 143-144
3 Donald McIntosh in some accounts
4 Abby Maria Hemenway, *Vermont Historical Gazetteer* (published by the author, Burlington 1867), I, p. 645
5 Governor and Council, pp. 245-246
6 *Ibid.,* p. 246
7 *Ibid.,* p. 217
8 *Ibid.,* p. 219
9 *Ibid.,* p. 222
10 *Ibid.,* p. 228
11 *Ibid.,* p. 252
12 *Ibid.,* pp. 252-253
13 A.M. Caverly, *History of Pittsford, Vt.* (Rutland, Vt.: Tuttle & Co., 1872), pp. 132-133
14 *Ibid.,* p. 122
15 *Ibid.,* p. 123
16 *The Public Papers of Governor Thomas Chittenden,* (Barre, Vt.: published by the State, 1969), pp. 434-436

## Chapter 4. The Expedition

1 Carleton to Haldimand, October 24, 1778 (PAC)
2 Powell to Haldimand, October 24, 1778 (PAC)
3 Carleton's Journal, p. 7 (PAC)
4 *Ibid.,* p. 8
5 *Ibid.,* pp. 8-9
6 Return of the Commissioned Non Commission'd Officers Drumrs & Private Going on the Expedition, Under the Command of Major Christopher Carleton (PAC)
7 Carleton to Haldimand, November 24, 1778 (PAC)
8 Powell to Haldimand, October 24, 1778 (PAC)
9 Carleton's Journal, p. 7
10 *Ibid.*
11 *Ibid.*
12 *Ibid.,* p. 8
13 *Ibid.*
14 *Ibid.*
15 *Ibid.,* p. 9
16 *Ibid.,* p. 10
17 *Ibid.*
18 *Ibid.*
19 Hemenway, I, pp. 12-13
20 Carleton's Journal, p. 10
21 *Ibid.,* p. 11
22 *Ibid.*
23 *Ibid.,* pp. 11-12
24 *Ibid.,* p. 12
25 *Ibid.*
26 *Ibid.,* pp. 12-13
27 *Ibid.,* p. 13
28 *Ibid.*
29 *Ibid.,* pp. 13-14
30 Hemenway, p. 382
31 Carleton's Journal, p. 14
32 *Ibid.*
33 *Ibid.*
34 *Public Papers of George Clinton, First Governor of New York* (Albany, N.Y., published by the State, 1899-1914), IV, p. 309
35 Carleton's Journal, pp. 14-15
36 *Ibid.,* p. 15
37 Swift, pp. 182, 184
38 Swift, p. 186
39 *Ibid.*
40 Henry Perry Smith, *History of Addison County, Vermont* (Syracuse, N.Y.: Mason & Co., 1886), p. 713
41 Return of Rebel Prisoners brought to Quebec December the 6th 1778 (PAC)
42 Hemenway, p. 69
42a *Ibid.,* p. 70
43 Carleton's Journal, p. 15
44 *Ibid.*
45 *Ibid.*
46 *Ibid.,* pp. 15-16
47 Josiah F. Goodhue, *History of the Town of Shoreham, Vermont* (Middlebury, Vt.: A.H. Copeland, 1861), pp. 151-158

# Appendices

48 Goodhue, p. 151
49 *Ibid.*, p. 152
50 *Ibid.*, pp. 151-152
51 Carleton's Journal, p. 15
52 *Ibid.*
53 Reprinted in *The Valley Voice* (Middlebury, Vt.), February 12, 1975
54 Carleton's Journal, p. 16
55 *Ibid.*
56 *Ibid.*
57 *Ibid.*
58 *Ibid.*, p. 17
59 *Ibid.*
60 *Ibid.*
61 *The State of Vermont, Rolls of the Soldiers in the Revolutionary War 1775 to 1783,* compiled and edited by John E. Goodrich (Rutland, Vt.: The Tuttle Company, 1904); also Abby Hemenway, p. 66
62 David W. Hoyt, *A Genealogical History of the Hoyt, Haight, and Hight Families* (Providence: printed for the author by the Providence Press Co., Boston: Henry Hoyt, 1871), p. 51. We are also indebted to William Hoyt of Rockport, Massachusetts, and to Harold Carr of Charlotte, Vermont, for sharing information about the Hoyt family with us.)
63 Hemenway, p. 66
64 Carleton's Journal, p. 17
65 *Ibid.*, p. 18
66 *Ibid.*
67 *Ibid.*
68 Governor Clinton Papers, IV, p. 309
69 Hemenway, pp. 581-582
70 Swift, p. 89
71 *Ibid.*
72 Hemenway, p. 82
73 W.S. Rann, *History of Chittenden County, Vermont* (Syracuse, N.Y.: D. Mason & Co., 1886), p. 536
74 Return of Rebel Prisoners
75 Carleton's Journal, p. 18
76 Powell to Haldimand, November 11, 1778 (PAC)
77 This may be the Henderson mentioned on p. 51
78 Carleton to Haldimand, November 14, 1778 (PAC)
79 Haldimand to Carleton, November 19, 1778 (PAC)
80 Carleton to Haldimand, November 24, 1778 (PAC)
81 Carleton to Powell, December 29, 1778 (PAC)
82 Haldimand to Germain, March 2, 1779 (PAC)
83 Powell to Haldimand, January 17, 1779 (PAC)
84 Haldimand to Carleton, January 21, 1779 (PAC)
85 Powell to Haldimand, November 15, 1778 (PAC)

## Chapter 5. The Prisoners

1 Swift, pp. 90-91
2 *Ibid.*, p. 86
3 *Ibid.*, p. 91
4 Petition by Peter Ferris (PAC)
5 Thomas Sanford to wife, no date (PAC)
6 John Nairne to Captain Matthews, May 14, 1780 (PAC)
7 Swift, pp. 87-88
8 Hemenway, p. 363
9 Swift, pp. 91-93
10 John Nairne to Maj. Le Maistre, May 26, 1780 (PAC)
11 Swift, p. 86
12 Return of Rebel Prisoners brought to Quebec, 19 August 1781 (PAC)
13 Petition of Claudius Brittell, September 15, 1782 (PAC)
14 Swift, p. 86
15 Hemenway, pp. 82-83
16 Leon V. Bushey, *History of Monkton, Vermont,* (1961), pp. 15-16
17 Hemenway, p. 645
18 Lether of Richard Murray to Captain Matthews, Quebec, 25 May 1782 (PAC)
19 Letter from Matthews to Lieutenant Arbuthnot, Montreal, 20 May 1782 (PAC)
20 Richard Murray to Lieutenant Arbuthnot, 22 May 1782, Montreal (PAC)

# Carleton's Raid

21 Matthews to Murray, 20 May 1782, Montreal (PAC)

22 Captain Matthews to Officer Commanding at Three Rivers, Montreal, May 20, 1752 (PAC)

23 *Revolutionary War Rolls,* Vt., p. 791

24 *Hoyt Genealogy,* pp. 161-162.

Appendices

## THE RECORDS

# I

## *Carleton's Journal*

On Saturday the 24th of October at half past six in the morning, I left the Isle aux Noix; the Wind fresh down the Lake with small rain, prevented our getting on very much; with great difficulty I reached the upper end of Isle a Motte where wee encamped. most of the Indians arived soon after. *Sunday the 25th* I was detain'd untill Eight oClock in the morning waiting for the last of the Indians, I feared if I went on without them they might turn back, as I was inform'd they were not pleas'd with coming so far the night before. wee all moved off together and proceeded untill Six in the Evening, I encamp'd half a mile up Sandy Creek. the Gun Boats not being able to get over the Bar I orderd them into the next Bay half a Mile further on and directed them to get under way at one in the morning and as there was an appearance of a fair Wind desired them to proceed to Gilliland Creek there to remain untill I arrived. As the Maria lay in the mouth of the Bay I knew them to be in perfect security should I not be able to get so far that nighte, and they could not have been so well conceal'd in any other place.

A Mr Campbell came in haveing seen the Gun Boats as he was padeling in a small Canoe along Shore. he inform'd me that for certain I had been expected five weeks before at Rutland, that Whitcomb's post was Augmented to five hundred men, that Colonel Warner with two hundred was at Fort Edward, and that all the Militia was orderd to be ready at a moments Warning.

*Monday the 26th* . . . I sett off at two in the morning and reachd a deep Bay behind flatt rock Point, a little before sun rise. I orderd the detatchment to be in readiness to embark before dusk, but it blew so fresh from the S.W. that it was imposible to Stir nor could I send off a Canoe to procure me inteligence, which the information I received from Mr. Campbell rendered absolutely necessary.

*Tusday the 27th* . . . I had a field day to practice the men in the Wood fighting &c.

 After the field day I assembled the Indians Chiefs and told them my wish to send a person I could confide in to bring me a true State of the strength and situation of the Enemy. They saw the propriety of my proposal and consented to send the person I should pitch on for that service, in a small Canoe with five of their Young Men who were to go up without loss of time to the Vesel at Crown point, there remain untill dusk and under favour of the Night land him wherever he should think proper and return to the Vesel before light come down the Lake and Joyn me in the Evening. The person I sent was Mr. Johns, and at his request a Serjant of Captains Sherwoods Company with him. They expected to be in four days from their landing back at the place they sett out from; I made them lye down in the Bottom of the Canoe cover'd them over with a Blankett that they might not been seen. I intended to have moved off at dusk this Evening but the Wind coming round to the N.E. exceedingly fresh it was imposible to get our Boats of the Shore.

*Wednesday the 28th* . . . it continued to rain and blow very hard all day and night.

*Thursday the 29th* . . . Towards six oClock in the morning the Gale abated. a Field day at Ten oClock. about four in the afternoon the Canoe that had taken up Johns return'd. They had seen a Rebel Canoe which they Chas'd into Westbay, behind Crown Point but did not think it pudent to follow them. they reported the Carleton haveing left C. Point and fallen down to the mouth of Otter Creek which was contrary to my intention as I wish'd a vesel should be station'd there to prevent the Rebel Scouts rowing about in the Night by which means only they could discover my Approach. it became necessary I should remain where I was untill I could order the Maria up for that purpose. I requested the Chiefs to send two Scouts one to lye near the place where Johns was to come in at that he might not be pick'd up by any of the Rebel Scouts in case he return'd before the Maria got up to C. Point. The other to try and intercept the Canoe which had been seen by the first party. The two Scouts were accordingly sent.

*Friday the 30st* . . . a Soldier of the 29th Regiment was Kill'd by the Fall of a Tree. I sent early this morning to order the Maria who lay at Anchor about five Miles above me, to Take advantage of the first wind to run up to C. Point which she effected that Evening. I sett off at dusk and by two in the morning reach'd N.W. Bay I could not venture to pass this place without being Sure of reaching West Bay, as there was no intermediate one, where the Boats could be properly conceal'd.

*Saterday the 31st* ...in the course of the Evening of this day, both Scouts return'd and brought no intelegence, The night was so remarkably clear that I could not venture to Sett off untill past twelve, wee proceeded up with so much Silence that wee pass'd within half a Mile of the Maria without her hearing or seeing us altho' She expected us up. Wee reach'd the bottom of West Bay at four in the morning 1st of Novr. I informed Mr. Alder of our arrival there. I received a letter from him acquainting me that seeing some people in a House on Chimney Point he got under way, ran close in Shore and sent his Boat to bring them off; they proved to be four Inhabitants of Otter Creek Daniel McIntosh, David Stowe, Nathan Grizell, and James Henderson I directed that they should be detain'd Prisioners on Board, as I knew they could come there for no other purpose than to pick up Intelegence. I went on board to examin them but could not get any thing out of them. McIntosh I have since found told me very Great untruths, and he knew them to be such at the time. I sent a party in the Evening to wait Johns return.——

*Monday the 2d Novr* ...Sent fresh Scouts to different parts of the Country. at twelve one of them returned with a Benjamin Everest, I desired him to be conducted to the Main Guard, and that no person Should be allowed to come near him or Speak to him. I followed in less than five mints but before I reach the Guard he made his escape I made use of every means to catch him but without Success. some of the Indians did not return from the pursuits untill late the next day. A Scout of three Indians which I had sent to the mountains opposite my Camp Saw two Rebels on the Top of one of them, but could not take either of them. I imeaditly assembled the Chiefs, told them I feard our being there was no longer a Secret and that there was not a momente to be lost in Setting about whatever wee determin'd to attempt, that in the uncertainty I was in Relative to the Strength of Whitcombs Post, I would not touch it, but thought it advisable for me to march with the Greatest part of my detachment by a route which I Knew would carry me in upon Otter Creek thirty Miles above the mouth, from whence I should proceed downwards, that I wd. send Captain Fraser with thirty of their Young Wariors and 30 Rangers who should move up towards Pittsford destroying as they went on so that when they found it expedient to retire they would be able to march much faster untill they overtook me than any party sent in their pursuite could in prudence attempt. The Chiefs Approved my plan, and every thing was arranged for our departure next morning. at twelve at night Johns return'd, he said the reason he had been detain'd so long was, oweing to the absence of the person from whom he propos'd geting his Intelegence. he told me there were three hundred men at Rutland and two hundred at F. Edward, that the Arms of all the Inhabitants on the Creek were assembled at the BlockHouse, and that there were Seven hundred half Pounds of Powder with a proportion of Ball for that number of Militia in case of necessity, that Whitcomb had 44 single men as scouts on different parts of the Lake but that there was not the Smallest mention of our approach

One of my Scouts Sent out this morning not yet returnd.

*Tusday the 3d* . . . I was up by day light, Assembled the Chiefs and communicated the information I had received, which put them in Great Spirits about the plan determin'd on the night before only they thought it most advisable, not to Sett off untill the dusk of the Evening. at twelve the Scouts which had been sent out the day before in a Canoe return'd by land they reported that in the deep Bay to the Eastward of Sandy Battery, they perceivd two Rebel Boats containing about thirty men each which had passd them under favour of the Night; and seeing them padeling along Shore had cutt off their retreat by Water, they ran the Canoe on Shore and escaped by Land. They said also, that they had seen several large Smokes at the Saw Mill near Ticonderoga. I sent off Lieut. Houghton with some Indians and desir'd him to get a Satisfactory view of the Party so as to assertain—if Posible—their numbers and to try to get a Prisioner.

*Wednesday the 4th* . . . at one oClock Lieut. Houghton return'd saw no Apperance of any Fire or people in or near Ticonderoga but that with a Spy Glass he had discoverd the stern of a Batteau which was drawn up into some bushes in the deep Bay on the opposite shore where the Scoute was seen Yesterday, and two Men with Arms walking on the Beach. at 4 in the Evening I received a letter from Lieut. Aldery acquainting me that at one

Appendices

oClock, seeing a Canoe at one Smyths House on the East Shore two miles from Chimney Point he went in his Boat to enquire who She belonged to Smyth came runing down to the Water side and requested Mr. Alder not to land for that Scoute from Whitcombs Party at Ty. had left the House about twenty minnets before. I sent off fresh Scouts on each side the Lake with directions not to return untill they had either taken a Prisioner or were certain there were no detatchments there.

I sent an officer with Thirty Men to Secure Smyth and send him in to me and directed the Officer to take Post near the House so as to be Able to Surprize any Party that came to it. I also sent the two Gun Boats to cover the Party to prevent their being forced.

*Thurday the 5th* . . .at one this morning Smyth was brought in who informd, that a Lieut. Crook with one Ensign and Twenty five men had come there in two Boats the Night before, that they had a Birch Canoe with them which they Said they took that day from an Indian Scout, they Staid untill twelve oClock the next day at his House and haveing hid their Boats and Canoe, in a Creek close to the House were gon four Miles down the Lake that they Should be back that night that they were detatch'd from a Party which Whitcombe had near Ticonderoja.

I Suspected very much the Truth of all this Story as it was evident those Boats with the twenty five men were the two Boats with Sixty which the Indians Said they had been pursued by, and it was evident by their comeing in Boats they had come from Skeansborough and not Rutland I orderd a Captain with two Subalterns and forty Men with forty Indians to go off imeaditly to Surprize this party on their return; the Chiefs on being inform'd of my intentions agreed to it without hesitation and the party under the Command of Cap. Dixon of the 29th Regt. and Captain Fraser with the Indians sett off at two. at two in the Afternoon the detachment return'd, had been Seven Miles down the Lake but could not overtake the Rebel Scout as they had Struck off into the Woods towards Otter Creek and were Twelve hours a head of them. They brought in fifteen Prisioners Inhabitants on the Lake at dusk the Scoute from Ticonderoga Side returnd without seeing any appearance either by Tracks or Fires of any party haveing passd that way. At Ten oClock the Scout from mount Independance return'd with the Same report. I assembled the Chiefs to Know if they Approved of our setting off the next morning, and would attempt the excution of the first plan or thought it Necessary to adopt a new one. They would give me no answer untill they had consulted their young men that it was too late to let me have the answer that night but that I should have it next morning. A soldier of the 31st & 1 of the 53rd (both Germans) deserted this night. I sent after them & promised a reward but they got clear off.

*Friday the 6th* . . . I was up before day, Assembled a Councill and demanded their answer they said they thought it would be imprudent to Strike higher on the Creek than where I had propos'd going myself that they would go there if I would promise to take care of their Horses, which I consented to so far as lay in my power, they desired to Know what I would allow them a Head for the Cattle that might be taken I told them Eight Dollars for large Oxon, and in proportion for the smaller Ones. I consented to this in hopes it would prevent them from amusing themselves about other plunder & recommended the women & Children to their care to leave provisns for them.

I orderd a detatchment of two Captains (- - - - -) five Subalterns and one hundred men with Captain Jones and twenty Royalists for this expidition—Captain Fraser Lieut. Browne and Lieut. Houghton with the Indians: the two Mr. Frasers went as Volinteers. Captain Ross of the 31st Regiment as the Senior Officer on this expedition Commanded it. wee moved off at Eleven oClock. at two landed on the East Side two miles above Chimney Point and they sett forward imeaditly. At half past two I detached Lieut. Farquar with thirty Men and Cap. Sherwood as a Guide, for the purpose of burning Moors Sawmill. They were to go by water untill they got opposite to Putnams Creek, four miles above where I then was, there to land and proceed by a road which lead from thence Seven miles back to the Mill. I sent a Mattross with a Fireball least they Should not have time to Fire it in the usual way. I orderd Captain Dunlop of 53d with a Subaltern and Thirty men to Support Lt. Farquar with instructions to advance a party half way to the Mill for the purpose of reinforceing him if necessary, or facilitating his retreat in case of Accidents, haveing heard nothing of him by twelve at Night I concluded he had met no Obstruction I orderd Captain Dixon with twenty four men across the Lake to destroy Raymonds Mills.

*Saterday the 7th* . . . I sett off at day light and moved down the East

90

Side of the Lake destroying the different buildings as I went along but the Wind was so exceeding fresh at N.E. and haveing so few hands in my Boat I proceeded very Slowe at Twelve Captain Dixon Joyn'd me he reported haveing found a large quantity of Grain and fflour in the buildings adjoyning to the Mill all of which he effectualy destroyed.

At two Captain Dunlop overtook me he inform'd me that he had gon with Lieut. Farquar himself, that they had proceeded withouth interuption to a House within five hundred Yards of the Mill, that a Party of Rebels Posted in this House Fired upon him he form'd his detatchment and after an engagement of about twenty minnets the Rebel Firing ceas'd intirely. That from their Cries he had reason to belive numbers of their Men had been Wounded he drew off his Party and return'd to his Boats with one Man Wounded he concluded that the Party he had met had been the advanced Guard of a detatchment in the Mill and it beeing Night thought it it imprudent to Hazard beeing Sorrounded in the Woods by Superior numbers.

It was not in my power to proceed further than Buttmold bay this Evening.

*Sunday the 8th* . . . Detatched a Scoute of five Indians to bring me intelegence if there was any troops in the Blockhouse at the first Falls on Otter Creek; with directions to examin both Shores as they went up least the Rebels Should be conceald there I moved off at Eight halted at the mouth of Creek an hour then proceeded on with the two Gun Boats and the Batteaus, at 3 I met the Scout who brought in two Prisn. by whome I was inform'd that there were no Rebel troops in that part of the Country nor had they seen any thing of Captain Ross's Approach. I halted at dead Creek four miles from the mouth of Otter Creek and threw an Abbattis round my Camp.———at 7 I saw Fraser's Fires and Shewd them to the Indians who seem'd to doubt it but consented to send a Scout to see, they return'd at 12 had seen Lamott with the Ottawas Indians who inform'd them that their ffriends were two Miles higher up the Creek.

*Monday the 9th* . . . I sent back the two Gun Boats with orders to make the best of their way down to the Isle Aux Noix I sett off at 7 and at ten arived at the falls four miles from dead Creek I found that Captain Jones with his Twenty Men had been detatched agreeable to my directions to destroy the TownShip of

Moncktown which lay Eight miles back paralel to the Lake my principal motive for destroying this Township tho' it delay'd me twelve hours was because I Knew it to be a remarkable rich one and a Nest of the Greatest Rebels in that part of the Country besides if I could be fortunate enough to Catch Wintress Howick the Indian Interpreter the only person who negociates the Congress business with the Villiages in Canada from thence I should do an esential Service. At 4 oClock Captain Jones return'd with Several Prisioners of which Howick was one he destroy'd a Consideriable Quantity of Arms Amunition Grain Forrage &c and brought off twenty four head of Cattle I sent the Cattle by land to the mouth of the Creek and moved down with the Detatchment in the Boats wee got to our Camp by Eleven oClock.

*Tusday 10th* . . . Employ'd all the morning in Ferying the Cattle to Split Rock. I orderd Mr. Lorimier down to Split Rock to see if the Indian Accounts of the numbers they brought in was Just Viz. Sixty Head, which with those brought by Cap. Jones Should amount to Eighty four or Ninety. At 2 they were all Ferry'd over I orderd the 31st detatchment to halt twenty four hours at Gililands Creek after the oxon were pass'd by, then to destroy the different Mills and buildings and proceed down the Lake. I orderd the Lee Cutter to cover this detatchment. The Maria was orderd to proceed down to Point aufer haveing no further occasion for her. I with the remainder of the detatchment and the Carleton ran down the East Shore in order to destroy the Buildings &c that wee might find on that Side. The Whole moved off at 4 in the Afternoon I left provis. & a large Rebel Batteau which I had taken, to Carry the Women and Childerin round to

Skeansborough the fineness of the Night tempted me to proceed on *the 11th* . . . about 2 in the morning it Grew so dark and blew so very fresh at S.W. that it Seperated the Boats. I put into Grand Isle with 2 more Boats and waited there untill one in the Afternoon. and seeing five Boats I push'd off I got down to Point aufer by dusk.____

*Thursday 12th* . . . left Pt. Aufer at 10 oClock and reach the Isleand at one.

*Friday 13th* . . . the remainder of the Boats except one came in. That Boat had on Board the Indian presents with a Serjeant and twelve

# Appendices

Private of the 29th and a Serjeant and one Private of the 53d Regiment.

Chr. Carleton
Major 29th Regiment

Isle aux Noix
    14th of Novr. 1778

# II

## *List of Prisoners sent to St. Johns by Major Carleton / 29th Regiment*

Derrick Webb
Wintress Herrick-Indian Interpreter
Elis Roberts
John Bishop
James Bishop
Clawdiss Brittal
Isaac Fananam
Clawdiss Brittal
Timothy Bishop
John Grizall-released & sent back with the women on account of his age being upwards of 70
Dieran Roberts
Clark Store
David Grizall
Adaniga Grizall
Jestes Studivent
John Grizell
David McIntosh
David Stowe
Nathl. Grizall
Peter Ferris
Squire Ferris

Nathl. Smith
Marshal Smith
John Ward
Benjn Pain
Johnan Dakes
Joseph Everest
Geo. Spaldin
Joshua Oakum
Fenis Oakum
Joseph Oakum
Fenis Oakum
Eliza Oakum
Ordel Squires
Eslay Squires
Eazolez Everist
Phillip Spaldin
Benjamin Webster
Ths. Sanford
Jams. Boddington

*Chr. Carleton*
*Major 29th Regiment*

# Prisoners brought to Quebec, December 6, 1778

| Names | Ages | When & Where taken | | |
|---|---|---|---|---|
| Justice Sturdisant | 37 | 8 Nov 1778 | New Haven | Otter Creek |
| Winter Howett | 39 | 9 Ditto | Monckton | Ditto |
| Adonijah Griswold | 20 | 8 Ditto | New Haven | Ditto |
| David Griswold | 17 | 8 Ditto | Ditto | Ditto |
| Elias Roberts | 42 | 8 Ditto | Ditto | Ditto |
| Nathan Grizzel | 22 | 7 Ditto | Ditto | Ditto |
| Duncan Roberts | 15 | 8 Ditto | Ditto | Ditto |
| John Bishop | 21 | 9 Ditto | Monckton | Ditto |
| Timothy Bishop | 17 | 9 Ditto | Ditto | Ditto |
| Claudius Brittal | 16 | 8 Ditto | Weybridge | Ditto |
| Claudius Brittal | 47 | 8 Ditto | Ditto | Ditto |
| John Bishop | 48 | 9 Ditto | Monckton | Ditto |
| Clark Store | 15 | 8 Ditto | New Haven | Ditto |
| John Griswold | 27 | 8 Ditto | Ditto | Ditto |
| Isaac Bennen | 35 | 8 Ditto | Ditto | Ditto |
| Derrick Webb | 48 | 8 Ditto | Ditto | Ditto |
| Philip Spalding | 23 | 4 Ditto | near Crown Point | |
| John Ward | 17 | Ditto | Ditto | Ditto |
| Thos. Sandford | 39 | 25 Octr. | Ditto | Ditto |
| Squire Ferrers | 14 | 1 Novr. | Ditto | Ditto |
| Peter Ferrers | 53 | Ditto | Ditto | Ditto |
| George Spalding | 17 | 4 Ditto | Ditto | Ditto |
| Joshua Hokam | 23 | 5 Ditto | Ditto | Ditto |
| John Oaks | 23 | 5 Novr. 1778 | near Crown Point | |
| Hordel Squire | 56 | Ditto | Ditto | Ditto |
| Marshal Smith | 23 | 4 Ditto | Ditto | Ditto |
| Martin Smith | 26 | Ditto | Ditto | Ditto |
| Isley Squire | 17 | Ditto | Ditto | Ditto |
| Benjamin Pain | 31 | 5 Ditto | Ditto | Ditto |
| Phineas Holkum | 52 | Ditto | Ditto | Ditto |
| Pineas Holkum Junr | 27 | Ditto | Ditto | Ditto |
| Joseph Holkum | 16 | Ditto | Ditto | Ditto |
| Elisha Holkum | 15 | Ditto | Ditto | Ditto |
| David Stow | 42 | Ditto | Ditto | Ditto |
| James Bodington | 24 | Ditto | Ditto | Ditto |
| Ben: Webster | 38 | 7 Ditto | Lake Champlain | |
| Joreal Aves | 18 | Ditto | Addison | Ditto |
| Isaac Kelloch | 23 | 5 Augst. | on board the Carlton Schooner | |
| Joseph Evest | 23 | Ditto | Ditto | |

*Rich: Murray*
*Comr of Prisns*

94

## List of buildings and supplies destroyed in the raid

Return of Buildings &a destroyed by the Detachment under Major Carleton in November 1778.

| | Saw Mills | Grist Mills | Dwelling Houses | Empty Houses or Barns | Barns full of Wheat | Stacks of Wheat | Stacks of Hay |
|---|---|---|---|---|---|---|---|
| From Chimney Point towards Ticonderoga on the North Shore | ,, | ,, | 8 | 5 | 1 | 1 | 6 |
| From Chimney Point to Button mould Bay on the East side of the Lake | ,, | ,, | 13 | 7 | 4 | 20 | 40 |
| On the West side of the Lake at Reymonds Mill | ,, | 1 | 1 | 2 | ,, | ,, | 1 |
| N: B: Upwards of 200 Bushels of Wheat & Flower—And the Buildings for a Saw Mill | ,, | ,, | ,, | ,, | ,, | ,, | ,, |
| On Otter Creek from the Mouth 25 Miles up. 1 Blacksmiths Shop 1 Block House and 1 Log House Loop holed for the deffence of the Ford over the River about 18 Miles up As also | 1 | ,, | 15 | 13 | 7 | 5 | 20 |
| At Monkton a considerable Number of Fire Arms. some Ammunition and | ,, | ,, | 5 | ,, | 5 | ,, | 5 |
| On the East side Lake Champlain from Otter Creek down | ,, | ,, | 5 | ,, | 4 | 2 | 3 |
| | 1 | 1 | 47 | 27 | 21 | 28 | 75 |

N.B. a Considerable number of Horses and a very great number of Hogs kill'd—about 100 Head of Horned Cattle kill'd or brought away.

*Chr. Carleton,*
*Major 29th Regiment*

# BIBLIOGRAPHY

Bradley, A.G., *Lord Dorchester* (London: T.C. and E.C. Jack; and Toronto: Morang and Co., Ltd., 1907)

Bushey, Leon V., *History of Monkton, Vermont* (1961) — no publisher listed

Carleton, Major Christopher, *Journal* (PAC)

Caverly, A.M., *History of Pittsford, Vermont* (Rutland, Vt.: Tuttle & Co., 1872)

Goodhue, Josiah F., *History of the Town of Shoreham, Vermont.* Published by the town. (Middlebury, Vt.: A.H. Copeland, 1861)

Haldimand Papers, The Public Archives of Canada, Ottawa

Hall, Hiland, *The History of Vermont from its Discovery to its Admission into the Union in 1791* (Albany, N.Y.: Joel Munsell, 1868)

Hemenway, Abby Maria, *Vermont Historical Gazetteer* (Published by the author, Burlington, Vt., 1867)

*Letters of Brunswick and Hessian Officers during the American Revolution,* (trans. by William L. Stone (assisted by August Hund), (Albany, N.Y.: J. Munsell's Sons, 1891)

McIlwraith, Jean N., *Sir Frederick Haldimand* (Toronto: Morang & Co., 1910)

Peckham, Howard H., *The War for Independence. A Military History* (Chicago, Ill., University of Chicago Press, 1958)

*Public Papers of George Clinton, First Governor of New York* (Albany, N.Y.: published by the State, 1899-1914), IV

*The Public Papers of Governor Thomas Chittenden* (Barre, Vt.: published by the State, 1969)

Rann, W.S., *History of Chittenden County, Vermont* (Syracuse, N.Y.: D. Mason & Co., 1866)

*Records of the Council of Safety and Governor and Council of the State of Vermont* (Montpelier, Vt.: published by the State, 1873)

Smith, Henry Perry, *History of Addison County, Vermont* (Syracuse, N.Y.: D. Mason & Co., 1886)

Swift, Samuel, *History of the Town of Middlebury in the County of Addison, Vermont,* to Which is Prefixed a Statistical and Historical Account of the County (Rutland: Charles E. Tuttle Company, 1971: reprint of first edition, Middlebury, Vermont: A.H. Copeland, 1856)

Appendices

# LIST OF MAPS

The map used decoratively on the dust jacket and throughout the book, and as an underlay on pages 44, 48, and 52, is a portion of a survey map made in 1796 by James Whitelaw, Surveyor General. The original is in the Wilbur Collection of Vermontiana, Bailey Library, University of Vermont. All line maps and overlays were drawn by co-author Paul Washington and the sketches used as chapter ends were drawn by Ida M. Washington.

# Index

# Index

# Index

*" . . . there ar*

*upon the borc*

*Champlain, C*

*about Ticond*

*Point that mc*

*conveniences*

*which would*

*approach of c*

FREDERICK

*Governor-C*